DAKOTAH

Also by Charles Bowden

Killing the Hidden Waters (1977)

Street Signs Chicago:
Neighborhood and Other Illusions
of Big-City Life, with Lewis
Kreinberg and Richard Younker
(1981)

Blue Desert (1986)

Frog Mountain Blues, with Jack W.
Dykinga (1987)

Trust Me: Charles Keating and the
Missing Billions, with Michael
Binstein (1988)

Mezcal (1988)

Red Line (1989)

Desierto: Memories of the Future
(1991)

The Sonoran Desert, with Jack W.
Dykinga (1992)

The Secret Forest, with Jack W.
Dykinga and Paul S. Martin (1993)

Blood Orchid: An Unnatural
History of America (1995)

Chihuahua: Pictures From the
Edge, with Virgil Hancock (1996)

Stone Canyons of the Colorado
Plateau, with Jack W. Dykinga
(1996)

Juárez: The Laboratory of our
Future, with Noam Chomsky,
Eduardo Galeano, and Julián
Cardona (1998)

Eugene Richards, with Eugene
Richards (2001)

Down by the River: Drugs, Money,
Murder, and Family (2002)

Blues for Cannibals: The Notes
from Underground (2002)

A Shadow in the City: Confessions
of an Undercover Drug Warrior
(2005)

Inferno, with Michael P. Berman
(2006)

Exodus/Éxodo, with Julián
Cardona (2008)

Some of the Dead Are Still
Breathing: Living in the Future
(2009)

Trinity, with Michael P. Berman
(2009)

Murder City: Ciudad Juárez and
the Global Economy's New Killing
Fields, with Julián Cardona
(2010)

Dreamland: The Way Out of Juárez,
with Alice Leora Briggs (2010)

The Charles Bowden Reader,
edited by Erin Almeranti and Mary
Martha Miles (2010)

El Sicario: The Autobiography of
a Mexican Assassin, with Molly
Molloy (2011)

The Red Caddy: Into the Unknown
with Edward Abbey (2018)

DAKOTAH

THE RETURN
OF THE FUTURE

Charles Bowden

FOREWORD BY TERRY
TEMPEST WILLIAMS

University of Texas Press
Austin

3|70
$25

Lannan
CHARLES BOWDEN PUBLISHING PROJECT

Requests for permission to reproduce material from this work should
be sent to:
Permissions
University of Texas Press
P.O. Box 7819
Austin, TX 78713-7819
utpress.utexas.edu/rp-form

♾ The paper used in this book meets the minimum requirements of
ANSI/NISO Z39.48-1992 (R1997) (Permanence of Paper).

Library of Congress Cataloging-in-Publication Data

Names: Bowden, Charles, 1945-2014, author. | Williams, Terry
Tempest, writer of supplementary textual content.
Title: Dakotah : the return of the future / Charles Bowden ;
foreword by Terry Tempest Williams.
Description: Austin : University of Texas Press, [2019] | Includes
bibliographical references.
Identifiers: LCCN 2019002903
  ISBN 978-1-4773-1996-3 (cloth: alk. paper)
  ISBN 978-1-4773-1997-0 (library e-book)
  ISBN 978-1-4773-1998-7 (non-library e-book)
Subjects: LCSH: Great Plains—History. | Great Plains—Social
conditions. | United States—History. | Indians of North America—
History. | Frontier and pioneer life—Great Plains. | Bowden,
Charles, 1945-2014—Family. | Bowden, Charles, 1945-2014—Travel.
Classification: LCC F591 .B69 2019 | DDC 978—dc23
LC record available at https://lccn.loc.gov/2019002903

doi:10.7560/319963

Foreword: Two Worlds

TERRY TEMPEST WILLIAMS

Americans think they can change their life. Americans think "I will move here and be a different person." Americans are on a false quest. The only voyage of discovery is to go back where you started. It isn't to flee something, it is to face something and comprehend it.

CHUCK BOWDEN in conversation with Scott Carrier, December 26, 2005, Tucson, Arizona

Dakotah is the conversation I wanted to have with Chuck Bowden but never did. He answers the questions I wanted to know the answers to but never asked: Where did you come from? Who are your people? What were you like as a child? And how did you come to see and understand the world as, at once, a place of tender beauty and injustices?

"I live in a time when nations harden into fossils and humans retreat into memoirs," he writes in the opening chapter, "My Piece of Ground." Call *Dakotah* an anti-memoir, a rearview mirror of a book written by a quick-minded writer who believed these stories would deliver him into the future a little more whole because the time he was living in was breaking his heart.

Bowden had reported on so much darkness and deceit along the US and Mexican border: the women murdered in Juarez; the drug cartels and the border police and all the shadowy figures in between where nothing is as it appears. He felt a responsibility to report on the unreported. And in the case of the borderlands, he stayed longer, perhaps, than he wanted because he wanted to know who was directing the killing—but nobody could tell him. It eluded him. What he did find were the words that broke us open as readers, forcing us to confront the brutal nature of our own species and that violence and compassion are siblings.

Chuck Bowden never turned his back on hard stories. He sniffed them out and followed his nose, a reporter who knew how to track down a scent that smelled like a lie. And when he found the lies, he exposed them, all of them, in bareboned language of the desert itself, a landscape of buried secrets uncovered by the wind through time—the same desert that raised him after he left Chicago as a boy, allowing him to keep his own secrets and his one truth, "I have never belonged."

Dakotah is an intensely personal, relentless rendering of the past and a quiet reexamination of our future. Bowden is the outsider who seeks the insider who will talk to him, whether it is his father's sister sitting at her kitchen table sharing family lore or El Sicario talking about torture. He knows how to listen. He keeps their stories real, taut, tells them straight with verbs over adjectives; and often what he does say isn't what you want to hear. He shocks us into the realization that if we are alive than we must feel both the pain and the beauty of the times we are living in. After reading one of Bowden's stories, my heart hurts. *Dakotah* is no exception. The bubble of privilege and denial that says we get to close our eyes to the world's suffering, especially that which is next door, bursts in any book Chuck Bowden writes.

I am writing about Bowden in the present tense because he is alive on the page, even though he is dead.

Charles Bowden died in the desert from a heart attack on August 30, 2014, in Las Cruces, New Mexico. He began his work as a writer at the *Tucson Citizen* as a crime reporter. Max Cannon, a colleague of Bowden's at the now-closed newspaper, said, "He lived on his own terms to the extreme—he was a master wordsmith, a detective, a poet, a scholar, a gentleman rogue, and a fearless traveler into humanity's darkest places."

I often wondered how this loner and lover of truth, a great American writer of nonfiction, held it all inside. How did he bring bullets and blood, cocaine and corruption, and the cold-edged indifference of killers that he befriended into the light of language capable of still illuminating a fierce belief in our humanity?

"There are two worlds," Bowden writes in *Dakotah*. "The living one moving in the day and night through the grass and forests, cruising the rivers, coursing through the seas. The sky, also. And then, there is the world of noise talking money and ideas and patriotism and duties and hundreds of other lies. I am stranded between these two worlds, tugged by the murders and vices of my species and bound by every cell in my body to the stars and dirt and slobbering beasts that live ignored and yet persist."

What persists in *Dakotah* is the ground beneath our feet—what we stand on and stand for, and it begins with family in place. His kinsfolk's place is in the middle of America, the "Heartland": "So my father plows the fields, finds arrows and stone axe heads and treasures them and never speaks of the murders that happened down the hill. Like with the vanished beasts, there is a silence. All the bones coming out of the earth, all the pollen studies suggesting different floras and climates, all the vanished tribes of people speaking mutely through busted stone tools or pottery fragments. The sherry is served after dinner at high table and the gore is entombed in quiet books shelved on the oak bookcases."

Bowden creates parallel memoirs born out of the stratigraphy of histories from his own family's occupation of the prairie, his family who witnessed days when sandhill cranes blotted out the sun and who recognized: "You live, you love, you learn, you die, and let's hear no complaining. The death of a child meant more than the reports from the war. The soil underfoot had more power than the machines that pawed it into rows and crops. And in the woods all the mysteries waited and could not be explained."

The alternate chapters that focus on the dignity and conscious destruction of Native people who lived on the plains generations before and after his ancestors are juxtaposed against the mythologies perpetuated by historical figures such as Andrew Jackson, Lewis and Clark, Daniel Boone, and Wild Bill Hickok, who make shadowed appearances in Bowden's contrary memoir. He shows us that their contributions to racism and Indian removal, alongside the removal of wild lands and wildlife, are part of our personal history, too, and cannot be segregated from the deep wounds and collective historical trauma that brown and black people carry as they continue to confront a white America. A Seminole chief named Osceola "who fought US armies to a standstill in Florida" eventually died in US custody. Those who knew Osceola said he died from grief.

"There is little to do in my nation but talk about race and little talk about race that faces the dark ground that made us. There is a feeling that that was then and has little to do with the now, a sense that everyone should get over it and move on."

In *Dakotah*, we are allowed to stay in the tender grounds of a writer's becoming, not to have his childhood romanticized but considered as a place of both recognition and reckoning.

Chuck Bowden writes: "In that moment when a person first climbed up on a horse and rode, velocity increased a thousand percent and life became the wind in our face. We think velocity is new, change is new, and this vast tumult and wave of fear is new. And we are wrong. There has never been firm ground for our lives and our only balm has been a forgetfulness of the changes we have endured."

He shows us memory is fluid, not fixed, and belongs to all of us, with one shared certainty: erasure is our destiny.

"I was born to be erased.

"And accept this fact."

The beauty of *Dakotah* lies in the pleasure and pain of remembering what it means to be human. Simple things. Daily things. Things that are real, not abstract.

"My mother believed in the power of sweeping the floor and kneading bread.

"My father loved words and books and hand-rolled cigarettes and beer in quart bottles."

We learn the author receives a box of family memorabilia after his mother's death. He discovers a bundle of love letters between his parents, one bundle tied with a pink ribbon, the other with string. "Together they number maybe 150, almost all mailed between September 1, 1936, and mid-December." He didn't open them for over three years. "I finally opened them when I thought that just maybe they might help me understand my hunger for ground."

Bowden's instinct was correct. Within their letters they dream of a piece of land, a farm they will find and call "Rest Haven." In 1938, they do find their farm in Illinois, with "a fourteen-room stone house on 160 acres of pastures, fields, woodland and orchard." The descriptions of the familial village emerge, with relatives and "strays" and animals and miles to explore "the dirt" that is the bedrock of Bowden's ars poetica. This is a bare-boned love song to his childhood, unsentimental yet full of the smells of damp earth in the spring, thickets of hardwood in summer, and always the wind. "The plains, big, windy, an ocean of grass that refuses to reveal a center." The same plains for the Lakota of "endless bones."

"I am the bold toddler and the rebellious child. I take no discipline, I watch everything, and I suck in scent before words and words before speech."

In 1948, Jude Bowden writes to his brother Reddy that he is going to sell the farm and move to Chicago. Young Charles is slow to forgive him, never to be healed from being taken off the land. For the rest of Bowden's life he would be looking for his home ground.

"On a bend, I will see it, a piece of ground off to the side. I will know the feel of this place: the leaves stir slowly on the trees, dry air smells like dust, birds dart and the trails are made by beasts living free. The stars do not complain. They live, explode, die and and send no messages of regret." He goes on to say, "The wind seldom blows at this place and days are almost always sunny. I've never laid eyes on it but I know it is there. There has never been a moment's doubt about its existence. The place is as solid as rock in my mind. I have never belonged to a place or movement or belief. But I still look. On a bend, I will see it."

Dakotah is an unfinished manuscript. At least that's how it feels to me. At times, it feels like Bowden is writing in shorthand: call it a prairie haiku, his mind racing through his fingers as they are flying across the page. Open spaces are created. Stories are cut short. Maybe he intended to return, revise, and deepen. But the words stop. Maybe that's how all memoirs should end, as a mystery—that word, the last beautiful word of this tender, contemplative book: *mystery*. Do we ever really know any person, any place, or how any story ends?

Charles Bowden may never have belonged to "a place or movement or belief," but he did belong to a people who were decent and worked hard. He also belonged to a changing America and a community of writers who cared about justice for all, including all species, not just our own.

"Once, I think I was seven or so . . ." Bowden writes, "a red fox darted just ahead of me and disappeared so fast I had doubts that it really existed. And so I pushed on into the tangle of undergrowth, hoping against hope that I would somehow catch up and run with it through the woods.

"I kept a skin complete with the head of a red fox in my room, something given to me by a kinsman, and I would nuzzle it through the long dark days of winter."

This was the passage that allowed me to believe Chuck Bowden was always searching for what was good and dazzling and just beyond his comprehension, something beautiful and brave, mysterious and enduring.

He kept wandering, writing, looking in the shadows with a bird's-eye view for that fox, that bend in the river, that out-of-reach truth.

Dakotah is among the last of his heart-written books where we can follow his scent.

Vamos a ver lo que Dios nos da.
(Just to see what God would grant us.)

A NINETEENTH-CENTURY
MEXICAN BANDIT explaining why
he took up the life

We were not in the least alarmed when the Sioux really came into sight. Our composure was doubtless due to the fact that the warriors had been for some years dead, and were reposing on platforms of boughs, supported at the four corners by poles about eight feet high. On one of the tombs lay two bodies—a woman, decked in beads and bracelets, and a scalpless brave, with war paint still on the parchment cheeks, and holding in his crumbling hands a rusty shotgun and a pack of cards. Beneath the platform lay the skeleton of the favorite pony, whose spirit had accompanied his master's to the happy hunting grounds. A feeling of awe crept over us as we built in through the historic castles of the dead, when the Professor brought us down to the stern realities of science with a remark: "well, boys, perhaps they died of smallpox, but we can't study the origin of the Indian race unless we have those skulls."

C. BETTS, "The Yale Expedition," *Harper's New Monthly Magazine*, October 1871 (as quoted in Tim Flannery, *The Eternal Frontier: An Ecological History of North America and Its Peoples* [New York: Atlantic Monthly Press, 2001], 67).

those first ten thousand years of my life

I will try to explain how I stumbled to the ground and never
got up.
    I know you didn't ask.
    But I did.

My Piece of Ground

On a bend, I will see it, a piece of ground off to the side. I will know the feel of this place: the leaves stir slowly on the trees, dry air smells like dust, birds dart and the trails are made by beasts living free. The stars do not complain. They live, explode, die and send no messages of regret. Sometimes, as the darkness grows I can hear them, always a low hum but I never quite catch the melody.

I have never belonged.

I've cobbled together a life without a clear idea of a career. Money has been a fuel, not an interest. I've never felt aimless but often careless.

The wind seldom blows at this place and days are almost always sunny. I've never laid eyes on it but I know it is there. There has never been a moment's doubt about its existence. The place is as solid as rock in my mind.

I have never belonged to a place or movement or belief. But still I look. On a bend, I will see it.

I got my suitcase in my hand
Now ain't that a shame.

I live in a time when nations harden into fossils and humans retreat into memoirs. I have never belonged to my time.

For me there are no nations, and families are a thin skin quickly shed once flight from the prison of home became possible. There are two worlds: the living one moving in the day and night through the grass and forests, cruising the rivers, coursing through the seas. The sky, also. And then, there is the world of noise talking money and ideas and patriotism and duties and hundreds of other lies. I am stranded between these two worlds, tugged by the murders and vices of my species and bound by every cell in my body to the stars and dirt and slobbering beasts that live ignored and yet persist.

No meeting of my kind has ever mattered to me as much as a tree on the hillside in the grey light of dawn as the leaves go from black to green with the soft brushstrokes of the light.

A bat got into the house through an open door and in the early hours of morning I found it lying exhausted in the kitchen sink and I slowly watched it die when I released it outside.

That image I carry with me.

I can barely remember a single headline in my life.

I can remember the first chicken I decapitated.

I can remember the first fish I ripped the guts out of.

I can remember the warm sticking feeling of the entrails on the deer as it spilled out from the slit I'd made from the rib cage to the asshole.

I just can't remember when.

Like that girl and my hand slid down.

Like that first fist that hit my face.

But almost certainly, it was morning, I am one, maybe two, I'm out on the grass in the farmyard, sound of clucking in the air, cattle lowing from the barn, the scent of my mother in my nostrils from that moment she set me down and I rub the green blades and my little hand mashes them and my fingers go green.

I didn't want to get up, ever.

I suck my fingers and inhale.

This, I should note, becomes a habit.

I'm leavin' here today
Yes, I'm goin' back home to stay

I am told to always aim for the middle and fire every round.

I am told never to point a gun at someone except to kill them.

I am given a shotgun, a rifle and the pistol my uncle used to blow his brains out.

I am told never to believe the way killing is portrayed in the movies.

I am told never to give ground.

And always keep the gun loaded.

Then he sits back, guzzles his quart of beer, and falls silent.

That is my father on the family land ethic.

There is no question period.

I am born between two points: a stone axe head found in a plowed field and placed on a fence post by my father, and the scars of an ancient and huge glacial lake whose collapse helped feed and sculpt the great delta of the Mississippi River.

I was born to be erased.

And accept this fact.

The ground under my feet has always meant more to me than the people around me.

I have dreamed all of my life about a house down by the river where I will live out my days, let the land heal and grow ever more fruitful.

I have dreamed all of my life of burning this place to the ground and then departing into the dark of night while the flames lick the ground.

I am not about closure. I am about reopening wounds and slashing through the scar tissue to the place where the dreams sleep and wait to come back to life.

I whittle the end of a stick, slide on a marshmallow and roast it black over the small wood fire as lightning bugs glow in the dusk. Images float before me like a dream.

The Case jackknife is razor sharp from constant honing on a whetstone, the air rich with the smell of oil as I stroke the blade.

Shucking fresh corn, the rank odor on my hands as the dogs gather round full of hope and curiosity.

The staleness of a city apartment in winter, the fresh blast of aroma rising from straw, cow shit and the Holsteins entering the barn door in a precise order and then waiting to be hobbled and milked.

I inhale the scent of the weeds as I hack at them in the garden and embrace scent rising off the black earth into my face.

The breath of long-dead dogs floats serenely in my memories and in my heart. The coarse laughter of vanished aunts and uncles warms the coldest night for me. Lately, distant moments of afternoon or morning, long-ago smells and sounds and colors keep brushing against my face.

I am three and I think of old man Zeiger sitting on his porch in Chicago whittling dogs that he then stained. He would speak in halting English and this seemed normal for the time, an America where immigrants and foreign tongues were so common as to be unremarkable. For years, I had a small dog he placed in my childish hands, the body dimpled by the blade to simulate fur.

I keep remembering things of no consequence. The rush I feel as the smell comes off chickens roasting on the grill in the late afternoon, the chatter of women fussing in the kitchen amid the pies and vegetables and salads and bawdy talk, the sour smell wafting off the beers in the paws of the men, the laughter of my father at his own absurdity and in the distance, the hens clucking as they scratch and feed.

That guinea hen pausing just before it is going to peck out my sister's eye and the crack of the rifle as my mother on the back porch of the farmhouse cuts it down.

I have despised America's view of itself most of my life—the belief that we are a city on a hill shining grace and light onto other nations, that we only fight defensive wars, that we have solved the problem of class by pretending everyone is middle class. And that race is a detail in our long illustrious past.

Thirteen thousand years ago, a large meteor apparently struck North America and demolished many life forms. Paleo-Indian artifacts abruptly ended up in the layers of soil. Most of the mega-fauna suddenly disappeared. Fires raged and turned entire ecosystems to ash.

National identity is a fabrication and comes and goes with the vast migrations of peoples. When Hadrian built his famous wall the people north of the wall were not Scots and the people south of the wall were not English. And reading of the evidence of the human presence in Europe over the last ten thousand years makes me realize the continent has been a constant movement of people.

Hunger has pushed me to go into deep time, that place before my life began and before written language began, to plow the very soil of my world. And to stare into the slivers of life I have known in my family. This last fact surprises me.

There is a big box at my feet, one I have been avoiding for three years. It is the past that my mother flung into my present, things found after she died that she had hoarded during her hard journey. My father's mother and father stare up at me from an old photograph, one that was probably taken in the twenties or thirties. I know my grandfather died in '43, died angry since he was determined to outlast World War II and see his youngest son home from the killing ground. My grandmother died several years before that. I was born after they were both in the ground. She stares out with kindly eyes. She was never disturbed by anything, or spoke a harsh word. He looks like a bomb about to go off, his Stetson planted on his head, a coat, white shirt, and stained trousers. They stand in the doorway of some small rural home in Iowa.

These things are easy for me.

But there are these piles of letters, letters going back to World War I, and a neatly tied bundle of my mother's and father's love letters. I have never read a line of these. They have sat in the box in my storage shed as I crept slowly toward them.

Now I feel ready.

I look in the box and think of Pandora and I am grateful for what she unleashed on the tedium of the world. I reach down, stare at a postmark, notice the old worn quality of the print dress my grandmother wears in the photograph.

I've got no time for talkin'
I've got to keep on walkin'

American lives are supposed to have straight narratives ending in redemption. I don't believe lives are straight stories. And I don't believe in redemption. You can only be forgiven if you have not really had a life.

Nor do I think a life can simply be a place. All lives take place somewhere but all places are larger than the lives that scamper across them.

A life can have meaning without having a lesson.

My life is about dirt.

There are other things in the mix. No one can speak honestly of American ground without facing race. Before I am three, I am riding on the backseat of a car into Lemont, Illinois, as the adults state with pride that no black person can be in the town after nightfall. Before I am three, I am looking down from the farm at Romeoville, Illinois, where blacks were murdered and driven out in the 1890s. I am in the bayou below New Orleans in the fifties visiting kin of my aunt. I am sitting on the levee in Rosedale, Mississippi, in the sixties drinking moonshine with a black bootlegger. I see a notice filed by Andrew Jackson promising a reward for the return of his runaway slave. Like the ground itself, all these events are of a piece to me. The separations biographies insist upon—the life and the work—I deny.

Just as the breaking of the ice dike thousands of years ago in the valley below the farm where I was born happened yesterday for me. And the Kankakee Torrent still roars in my ears as it casts billions of tons of soil downstream to create the delta where I'll drink white lightning with the bootlegger.

Everything is held together by my mind and my mind is simply a tool for understanding my hunger for dirt. The distance between the gumbo of the delta and the hard winter ground of the Dakotas is zero for me.

*   *   *

I move upstream, paddle in the water. The current is weak, the banks green, brush leans over, beaver watch me pass.

I once bought a canoe, worked the abandoned rivers where rapids kept out boats and no one bothered to dredge and channel. The silence owns, the paddle slips into the water, executes the J stroke, lifts and returns to the front, slices back into the current, and never a sound. Bought a fiberglass model just for the added silence. Deer would come into view standing in the water and drinking and never hear the approach.

I was sure then. Enough days and nights, camping light, bag never warm enough, food no more than grub, black coffee before dawn, then push off, I was sure that the ground would come to hand, my hand.

Around each bend, I thought the place would be there, waiting by the side.

Heartland

The white baseball hits the black grill with a thunk. I pick it up and am hypnotized by the white leather and frayed red stitching. A boy suddenly appears on the top of the fence and I pitch the ball back to him. He vanishes back into the neighboring yard. The sun pours down, spring flowers flutter in the light breeze. I'm spun back into games I had forgotten, the hardness of a ball fresh out of the box, smell of the oil on the leather glove, the adults lined up to watch the Little League game, the umpire Irish and drunk shouting out balls and strikes at each pitch until some of the men have had enough and there is a dustup behind home plate. I remember the fresh-cut scent of grass in the outfield, a fly ball, and I wheel and run and make the catch of my life, cock my arm and make the throw of my life to nail a runner sliding into home. Later I sit on the back porch under the stars, the night warm and soothing, thinking life can be a dream for brief moments.

I never could bat worth a damn, but I did have that one catch and throw that fine summer day with the adults watching on, the umpire drunk, and the sun burning away all the bad things with a golden fire.

My mind now wanders often, but not really to my childhood. Those years seem to have little attraction for me. They function more as a gateway door opening up memory and then I tumble into scents, a bird streaking across the sky at sunset, the cool damp of morning with the grass wet under my feet, the acrid smell of powder as I knock down a rabbit on the edge of the plowed fields.

And dirt, more and more the dirt, crumbling in my hand and pulling me under to the lost worlds laid down by ancient seas and winds and floods.

My mind runs along a carpet of ground, up and down the Missouri River, the Mississippi drainage, the prairies, the plains, gas seeping from the bayous and wrapping around me.

For years, my parents wondered what dementia lurked within me because I would drift away in the middle of a meal or sentence or second and go to some place they knew nothing about and could not name. There is the river gouging through my head.

Andrew Jackson

The year 1830 finds President Andrew Jackson saying, "Our conduct toward these people is deeply interesting to our national character. Their present condition, contrasted with what they once were, makes a powerful appeal to our sympathies. Our ancestors found them the uncontrolled possessors of these vast regions. By persuasion and force they have been made to retire from river to river and from mountain to mountain. . . . That step cannot be retraced."He is speaking of driving the Indians from the United States and across the Mississippi into land then seen as empty and useless. My father died in a state where he was not born. As did my mother. As will I.

Alexis de Tocqueville watches from the banks of the Mississippi at Memphis as Choctaws move west as part of Jackson's Indian removal. He writes, "It was then in the depths of winter and that year the cold was exceptionally severe; the snow was hard on the ground, and huge masses of ice drifted on the river. The Indians brought their families with them; there were among them the wounded, the sick, newborn babies, and old men on the point of death. They had neither tents nor wagons, but only some provisions and weapons. I saw them embark to cross the great river, and the sight will never fade from my memory. Neither sob nor complaint rose from that silent assembly. Their afflictions were of long standing, and they felt them to be irremediable."

*   *   *

I remember the exact moment the land slipped from my grasp and the road and the violence took up all the space. It is a June morning in 1968 on the Mississippi Delta. The shack has furrows plowed right up to the walls. I push open the door. Two kids aged four or five sit on the floor, their short hair with that reddish tinge that comes from malnutrition. A television is on, the screen a snow of poor reception and faint forms barely detectable through this blizzard of interference.

The kids are hypnotized and do not stir at my entrance. Outside, the heat is coming on and haze of early morning burning away to the glare of midday.

I have been toying for days with moving here—the black soil of the ancient river deposits, the slow movement and grace of the people, the rich vowels falling off everyone's tongue, the golden light and green trees. Get some ground, there, on a bend, by the side of the road.

The windows are blocked by old cardboard, a torn car seat serves as the couch. Flies buzz over a dirty skillet by the sink.

I take it all in. Stand there for five, ten minutes.

The kids on the floor never stir or acknowledge I am there. The poverty is not new to me, I come from the border. But the stillness in their bodies frightens me.

This is my country and these are my people and if I stay here this will be facing me every moment, the black skin, the race line, the world we made and are told to abide.

I back out, softly close the door.

That is when the land moved past my reach and asphalt poured down my throat.

After that just the names change and no place is ever Walden.

But, just as now, I keep trying.

On a bend, off to the side, I will see it.

* * *

There is little to do in my nation but talk about race and little talk about race that faces the dark ground that made us. There is a feeling that that was then and has little to do with the now, a sense that everyone should get over it and move on. It is boring, and covered with dust, and lies on a shelf in an abandoned building, barely glimpsed in the long tunnel called past time.

There is an old newspaper notice, from 1804. "Advertisement for Runaway Slave" it says. The man promises $50 for the return of his property, and will toss on an extra ten bucks for each hundred lashes, up to three hundred blows with the whip.

The man is thirty-seven years old, a colonel in the Tennessee militia, and will become famous as the symbol of democracy. His name is Andrew Jackson. He dies owning one hundred and fifty human beings.

As a boy I visit his home, the Hermitage, and take in the scent of the forests of Tennessee. It is one of many visits to the South, a place I don't believe in, and I come from the North, a place I don't believe in, or from the West, a place I don't believe in.

No use for you to cry
I'll see you by and by
'Cause I'm walkin' to New Orleans

I'm going to need two pair of shoes
When I get through walkin' these blues
When I get back to New Orleans

The noise called news dies away.

Silence smothers everything. The people never mention this silence. But the fear is everywhere. Fear of failure, fear of losing the job, fear of losing the house, fear of falling ill, fear of love and fear of abandonment.

I smash the radio, sleep on the ground, bury the phone in a field between Sioux Falls and Cheyenne, toss the gun into a river, break the seal on the bottle as the tach climbs into the red.

On a bend, I am sure of it.

Off to the side.

And so I stay, as always, just as I am leaving, I always stay.

On a bend, I will see it, a piece of ground off to the side.

Lewis and Clark

They move slowly upstream. The Sioux are not to be trusted, no one questions this fact. The river itself offers sandbars and turbulence and sunken trees waiting like spikes to sink any craft. Captain William Clark jots down his new world on Saturday, October 13, 1804. They see a Sioux camp on their left but ignore it and then twenty-three miles upstream they pass a creek and it is called, in the captain's records, Chief Pocasse or possibly Hay and on the other shore, they see stones a few miles inland that have the look of two people accompanied by a dog. The Rickores, the captain notes, believe the rocks are a man who loved and a girl who was forbidden to marry him by her parents. And a dog joined them in their sorrow and then they all turned to stone. While their love became rock, they ate the wild grapes that grow on the site and Captain Clark notes a huge concentration of the best grapes he has ever seen.

The expedition is barely within what people later call North Dakota. They are heading to the distant ocean. So notes must be made, information gathered. A new world is being recorded, one that is old but no one knows quite how old. But all agree, the people in the boats moving slowly toward the distant ocean, and the people on the banks watching them with wary eyes, all agree the expedition brings the new and the old is somewhere on the shore and in the rocks that once were a man, a girl and a dog.

She is beautiful and everything a man wants except—and even this point is open for debate—except for the fact that her vulva is actually part of a squash blossom. It happens this way. She is pretty, she is young and her brothers tell her she should get married because someone will give many horses for her. And then a man's relatives come and ask for her and offer many horses and still she says no.

Her brothers ask her why she will not marry and she says nothing, but keeps saying no. Until she gives in and finally says yes to another man who sends his relatives offering many horses.

Of course, it is because of the flower growing between her legs with rich yellow petals. And a bee flies around inside that flower and she knows the bee is her husband.

So she marries and the squash blossom wilts.

That is the report: she feels shame, she goes off, the dog follows and they both gradually turn to stone.

That is the way the Arikaras—the tribe the captain writes down as Rickores—tell it. Clark hears a similar story only this time the man apparently follows, and also turns to stone. There is no report of her husband, the bee.

This is how it is before everything becomes new and breaks free of the ground and of time. There is this the before—stones that were people, women with squash blossom vulvae that flutter in the breeze of the prairie—and then a new kind of time begins. The ticktock of the clocks, and nations insist on their power and break all to their will.

She never will marry, she will be no man's wife, she will have a squash blossom flaming yellow between her legs as the wind ripples the fresh grass and the air rolls raw with the scent of rank growth along the river named Missouri and lives on and on, a pure thing still standing in a gone place.

They have hardly hit the water below Pittsburgh before the trouble starts. Meriwether Lewis and his men land at Brunot's Island. His friend lives there and so Lewis shows them his new toy, an air gun with the look of a Kentucky rifle. He hits his mark seven times at fifty-five yards and then turns the weapon over to a Mr. Blaze who fires it accidently. Forty yards out the ball passes through a woman's bonnet. She collapses, blood streaming from her grazed temple.

At first, Lewis thinks she is dead, but soon she revives and seems fine.

He boards his men immediately, heads downstream on the Ohio. He is Pacific Ocean–bound.

The air gun, useless for game, impresses tribes across the continent.

It is August 30, 1803, and the beginning of something and the end of something.

The Navajos have a legend where a hummingbird is sent to see what is found above the blue, blue sky.

He finds there is nothing there.

Dakotah

Until the end of the last ice age, the Missouri watershed pretty much drained north into Hudson Bay. A knife edge slices across North Dakota where the ice breathed down our ancestors' necks and fenced in their world. Then, with the last big melt, there were some changes. Now the waters feeding the Missouri float off the tongue with this roll call, Arrow Creek, Bad River, Belt Creek, Big Muddy Creek, Big Sioux River, Blue River, Boyer River, Cannonball River, Chariton River, Cheyenne River, Cow Creek, Crooked River, Dearborn River, Fishing River, Floyd River, Gallatin River, Gasconade River, Grand River in Missouri, Grand River in South Dakota, Heart River, James River, Jefferson River, Judith River, Kansas River, Knife River, Lamine River, Little Blue River, Little Missouri River, Little Muddy Creek, Little Sioux River, Loutre River, Madison River, Marias River, Milk River, Moreau River, Mosquito Creek, Musselshell River, Niobrara River, Nishnabotna River, Osage River, Papillion Creek, Plate River, Platte River in Missouri, Poplar River, Redwater River, Roe River, Sixteen Mile Creek, Smith River, Soldier River, Sun River, Tobacco Garden Creek, Vermillion River, White River, Wolf River, Yellowstone River, ah, yes, the Yellowstone River floating the steamboat with the few things left from Custer's last moment of command.

Heartland

Her grave stares from the edge of the valley in the sand hills, a place near the ranch where her father raised the family and warred against the world. Mari Sandoz is both the recorder and the victim of the ground, a child of Swiss immigrants. Born in 1896, the same year as my father, she was the oldest of six raised on a hard ranch. Her father enjoyed drink, bold talk, and when feeling bad about life, beat his wife. He corresponded widely, tried agricultural experiments, held a kind of stern salon in his isolated place, and, given his reputation as a good shot, served as a one-man defense unit for the farmers coming in and butting heads with the ranch culture. He also surveyed plots for the newcomers.

Mari learned English at nine when she finally made it to a public school—as did my mother a few hundred miles to the east in Iowa. She left home by marrying a cowboy and when that swiftly failed she went to Lincoln, starved her way to an education and worked on a book endlessly. It was about her father and called *Old Jules* and was finally published in 1935.

When as a child I would ask questions about my dead grandfather, I'd be told that all I needed to know was in *Old Jules*.

Sandoz eventually made it to New York City, lived in the Village and wrote histories of the Sioux and the land. The distance seemed to make this work more bearable.

I am in her sister's house in the Sand Hills, a small place surrounded by a belt of trees that looks to be under siege. Outside, the dunes, hidden under a carpet of grass, seem to roll on like an ocean. The house stands as a fort built against the land and the wind and the whiteouts of winter. It is not far to Wounded Knee but it is very far from what the settlers dreamed they would find.

The country feels mean when viewed from inside the house. But outside it feels like a fatal attraction. She pours coffee, talks of her sister, takes me downstairs and shows the books of Mari Sandoz I might buy. But the freshness is gone, the plains have been entombed in nice bound volumes by a woman who knew all the pain and all the scents. It is this way in the official stations of the thing called settlement—the museums, the paintings, most of the memoirs, the historical societies. Clean glass cases with oddments from brutal winters and children dying early and often. The dead buffalo are warm memories. Now herds of cattle eat down the grass, and the plains want to be cowboys, country and western music and strange hats worn by bankers in the stuffy air of their offices.

The insane women trapped in cabins in the wind with the sour smell of pent-up living are hardly remembered at all. When I was a kid, I could make no connection between the tales of pioneers and the kitchens where they were told as dinner simmered on the electric stove.

*   *   *

I find an old cedar box, a small half oval. I open it for the first time in half a century. It is from my childhood, some trove I kept that got stored for no reason when I left home. There are two full-jacketed rounds for my .303 Enfield. A dozen .22 Long Rifles. And clusters of wooden matches with the tips sealed and waterproofed by wax.

One cufflink.

And the paper case for two Marlin blades for a safety razor.

I fondle the cartridges, and suddenly ballistics tables that I pored over night after night march through my mind. I can see numbers detailing the range of the .264 Magnum I once craved as an antelope killer, a caliber now largely out of production, and the gleaming stock of a Weatherby, the dazzling bands of colors from different woods glued together in loud grandeur.

I find a tarnished penny stamped 1960 and a small piece of copper ore.

The ghost light is on, that faint glow that keeps people from tripping in the theater when the performance is over and the players and audience have departed.

I read history. When others deny the past, I am annoyed. When others claim it answers all the questions, I am appalled. The same with archaeology, theology, geology, anthropology and agricultural studies. I want all the explanations, epochs, theories to be gone. Just the thing itself left in the theater faintly peering out at me in the glow of the ghost light.

Like Daniel Boone, the woman with a bee and squash blossom between her legs, the clay soil I first touched as a child in Illinois, the floating wonder of fireflies at dusk, it beckons me to some place where things join and make a sense I have not yet found in the books.

Let the ghost light show the way.

*   *   *

They kill eight in June 1893 and all the others leave Romeoville. None return until the 1970s. That is how the little town down the hill from the farm got rid of black people, and forgot it had ever done this.

When I was a child I heard rough talk about black people, statements made without apology and without doubt. But I never heard of Romeoville, of that June day in 1893 when whites killed black people and drove the survivors out. This was in northeastern Illinois, on the ragged edge of the pall of smoke off Chicago.

I had no idea how segregation was maintained or why.

But I could not imagine how it could go on and on. It seemed an impossible task, like controlling the weather.

So my father plows the fields, finds arrows and stone axe heads and treasures them and never speaks of the murders that happened down the hill. Like with the vanished beasts, there is a silence. All the bones coming out of the earth, all the pollen studies suggesting different floras and climates, all the vanished tribes of people speaking mutely through busted stone tools or pottery fragments. The sherry is served after dinner at high table and the gore is entombed in quiet books shelved on the oak bookcases.

There were seventeen tribes in Iowa and then there are none. Father Jacques Marquette and Louis Joliet looked into eastern Iowa in 1673, Lewis and Clark came up the Missouri and found fat channel catfish, beaver, ducks and more pelicans than they could count. The land began to be thrown open at the end of the Blackhawk War in 1833. The people flowed into hardwood forests and fertile prairies. As late as the 1870s, two hundred whitetail deer could be seen in a day. But by 1900, they had vanished. The elk left in the hard winter of 1856–57, the bison killed out by the time of the Civil War.

By the mid-1950s, 95 percent of the wetlands had been drained and murdered, of the forests over 70 percent had been felled and 99.5 percent of the prairies were slashed by plows.

I am out there as a child and no one remembers the killing, the plowing, the swing of the ax toppling the trees. It is a picture by Grant Wood of perfect fields and fine farmhouses with lush kitchen gardens near at hand. It is a thing called the heartland without a wild heart.

Wood's work is an artful deception and his canvases —"American Gothic," "Stone City, Iowa"—capture wounds on the land. When I was a boy his prints hung in farmhouses all over the state and no one ever mentioned that though there is black earth and fine corn in his paintings the people portrayed never seem happy, as if the last train to paradise has already left.

In Cedar Rapids, I stalk his world. He has been buried alive in a tomb called regional painting. His painting of Paul Revere alerting the countryside captures a populace asleep at the switch.

As a boy, I dream of Lewis and Clark, handle the odd arrowhead that turns up in the fields after spring plowing. Everyone goes to the movies when a western plays. No wolf has howled on the Iowa prairie since 1910.

My father had his first good job in a county called Osceola, named after the Seminole chief who fought US armies to a standstill in Florida, then died in US custody. At the time, many thought he died from grief.

Jude

There is a small leather notebook with an embossed flag on the cover, three rings for holding the strips of paper that are two inches wide. The handwriting is clear and spidery.

"The 9th Chap of Mark shows that some devils are deaf and dumb.

"5 Chap of Acts shows difference between sickness and presence of a devil.

"20 Chap Revelations devil was to be released in 1000 years.

"There is the same difference between religion and science that there is between a mad house and a university; a fortune teller and a mathematician."

It goes on like that for pages marching through the Bible.

Then the pages go blank. And I know why because I know what happened in April 1917 and what few choices were open for men like him as the government rolled over them.

The little notebook is dated 3/15/17, Harris, Iowa. And signed with my father's name.

He did a few things yearly to steady himself. He read the Bible, also John Bunyan's *The Pilgrim's Progress*. He also read all of Shakespeare's plays annually.

And Charles Dickens's *Little Dorrit*, lest he ever forget.

A wind comes up within me, and I catch the breath of the sea, the stagnant rot of the slough pockmarked with muskrat homes, the green yearning of black earth on a spring day, the assault of dirt oozing through the ice and broken pavement in a Chicago alley on the morning of that first thaw.

I read that the skin on my body is one-thousandth the radius of my body and that the soil on the earth, this skin that mesmerizes me, is one ten-millionth the radius of our planet. There are more than 20,000 types of soil in the United States. Worms matter more than presidents. Charles Darwin, as he teetered on the edge of the grave, published his final book, a treatise on earthworms. At the time, it was seen by critics as proof of a declining mind. Darwin wrote, "It may be doubted whether there are many other animals which have played so important a part in the history of the world, as have these lowly organized creatures."

Civilization is seven to ten thousand years old depending on what yardstick is selected. It creeps out of the melting ice of the last glacial period and springs from the barley and wheat of Mesopotamia and from similar wild plants tamed for the household in other sections of the planet.

I have never believed civilization was permanent.

Heartland

My mother believed in the power of sweeping the floor and kneading bread.

My father loved words and books and hand-rolled cigarettes and beer in quart bottles.

My mother is out there working in the garden. The white chickens peck at the ground. I crawl and am dazzled by the rank smell coming off the tomato leaves as I twine them in my hand and am brought up short by the red in the thick stems of the rhubarb.

There is an old upright piano and music thunders through the stone house. The air inside is the soft scent of wood in the iron cook stove and the constant cigarettes and the sour aroma off the beer bottles. Crows call from the trees and savage the fruit. The light is golden as dinner cooks.

And soil. Clay soil up on the hill by the farmhouse, darker and richer ground down by the creek. All the while the worms are working, fat ones called night crawlers and smaller red ones when they cannot be found for bait. Each century they inhale soil, grind it up, shit it out and build a half inch to two inches of new ground. Darwin is entranced, he hurls his sons against the ruins of England, and they dig and find the floor of an abbey destroyed during the reign of Henry VIII, now six to twelve inches under the earth. A Roman villa lies buried by two and a half feet. All this work, this burying with soil results from the toils of earthworms. Darwin pauses and realizes this activity happens all over the world, is ignored and is essential. And so he publishes and is considered an old fool.

The ice has come seventeen times in the last 2.4 million years. North America had a bigger ice pack than the current frozen load on Antarctica. And given the 105,000-year cycle of ice maximums, the scientists see the new cold wave coming at any moment. Sixty-five million years ago, a meteor strikes southern Mexico and wipes out most forms of life.

When I was fourteen my dog went down with his hind legs paralyzed and I spent the summer sleeping on the floor by him and trying to salvage his life. He couldn't control his bowels or bladder and so we both lived on the tile floor of the bathroom. That was the summer I read the complete works of Francis Parkman, Frontenac Edition, sixteen volumes published in 1899 in blue cloth with titles pasted on the spines. I can still smell the pages from this, the saddest summer of my life, as my dog slowly declined and had to be killed. I learned the catechism of the course of empire.

Dakotah

I drive onto Hickok and smell the greed in the air of Deadwood as people pull the handles on penny and nickel slots. A man dressed as Wild Bill Hickok walks up and down the main street. He is killed several times a day, shot in the back of his head while playing cards. The announcement says, "Bring the kids!" On the road, buffalo slowly pass as I stand on the shoulder, the calves giving little hops and then flowing into the brown grass. Dead presidents stare from the rock of Mt. Rushmore.

A woman leans against the rail on the hotel roof and explains, "You know the people around here call Deadwood Deadweird."

Ella Watson, a struggling migrant, chances upon a dangerous place to homestead in Wyoming and becomes Cattle Kate. She is hanged for rustling and lingers in the records as a whore and foul-mouthed wench. None of this is true, save the hanging. The same fate meets Calamity Jane, Wild Bill Hickok, Charlie Utter, Gall and a smattering of others who fuel eastern dreams of western places. The plains, big, windy, an ocean of grass that refuses to reveal a center, an expanse and sensation more than a location, becomes a theater of fraud run by dime novelists, playwrights, historians, buffs and people who like to lick the blood off all the Wounded Knees.

In 1856, when Hickok is nineteen and living in Kansas, he writes his brother Horace back in Illinois, "I am a pilgrim and a stranger and I am going to wander.... I am getting to be a perfect hermit, my fiddle, my dog and my gun I almost worship. I hold no intercourse with the world around, everything looks dark about me and around but there is a bright spark ahead and it I see and it I pursue until my fiddle strings break, my dog dies and my gun bursts that is so ..."

He's been raised on cheap books about Daniel Boone and Kit Carson. And soon, within a few years, he too will become a cheap book sold in eastern cities. This West is made legend before anyone really has much notion of the ground or much experience of the life. Calamity Jane, whom Hickok barely knew, becomes a pulp legend at age twenty-two while on an early foray into the Black Hills. In both cases, the fictional tales take over the actual life. Hickok is portrayed as both hero and cutthroat, a man who killed hundreds. Calamity is a heroine, a pony express rider and has other roles. In her own life, she washed clothes, was a sometime prostitute, raised two children, drank a lot and died at age forty-seven, a legend because of dime novels she could never read since she was illiterate.

Hickok begins as a clean thing, an Illinois farm boy who loves to go into the woods and hunt, a habit that a century earlier branded Daniel Boone forever. Like Boone, he hails from righteous stock—Hickok's people devote themselves to the underground railroad, trundling slaves toward freedom. He practices shooting, becomes a crack shot with a pistol, kills a few people but mainly likes to gamble (he loses), drink and mind his own business. He is a person with no need to kill and little hesitation when the killing time comes.

On the ground, lives play out as tiny appetites, not grand themes. Martha Canary, better known as Calamity Jane, is orphaned as a teenager, becomes a camp follower as the Union Pacific puts down rails across Wyoming in the late

1860s, and soon is drinking, smoking and fucking for money. In an eighteen-month period, Wyoming goes from about a thousand people to thirty-five thousand, most living in huts and barely staying alive. In 1874, she is smuggled into the Black Hills as part of a military expedition (the boys dress her in male gear so she can tag along). A few news stories transform her into Calamity Jane.

Two years later in July 1876, she hitches a ride on a wagon going to Deadwood with Wild Bill Hickok, has a glancing acquaintance with him for a few weeks until Jack McCall blows his brains out on August 2. Years later, after appearing in Wild West shows and having a hack write her autobiography, Martha Canary dies and so locals think it would be a nice thing to bury her next to Hickok in Deadwood. And so it is done and they become an item in eternity.

Long after Hickok is murdered scholars poring over ancient documents conclude that Wild Bill's ancestors may well have been tenants of William Shakespeare. More interesting is that in 1854 when Hickok is a seventeen-year-old teamster in Illinois he sees his boss abusing horses and tosses him in a canal. Hickok is fired. He becomes a man with many tales attached to his name but hardly any suggest meanness. He weds a woman who rides horses in the circus, is a tightrope walker and also the owner of the show, earning $5,000 a year. He seems to have gone to Deadwood to earn a stake of some kind so that he could measure up to her success.

His custom is to sit with his back to the wall in poker games. But on this day when he asks other players to change their seats they make fun of him and so he finally takes a chair with his back to the room. It is a little after noon when Jack McCall fires into the back of his head and Hickok pitches backward in his Prince Albert frock coat. McCall then tries to shoot a few more people but his gun misfires. He goes out back and mounts someone's horse and promptly falls off because the cinch has been loosened. No one ever really finds out why he killed Wild Bill, and the following year he is hanged in Yankton, Dakota Territory.

Hickok falling backward from his seat in the saloon, the dead man's cards scattering on the floor; he has the easy out. Calamity Jane spends the rest of her life scuffling and peddling photographs and pamphlets about herself.

Everyone becomes dime novels, quick little books for American boys and laborers that have press runs of sixty thousand, multiple readers.

*　*　*

The first Sioux, also called Lakota, Nakota, Dakota, saw the Black Hills in 1770. They had been driven from Minnesota by the Ojibwa, among others. In time the Sioux drove the Kiowa from the Black Hills and assumed possession. Then, in the 1870s, a prospector and the US Army broke the hold of the tribes and the hills became for a tiny moment a way station of Wild Bill and Calamity Jane.

Gall is a chief of the Hunkpapa Lakota, and for years he is a key man in Sitting Bull's efforts to stave off white penetration. They were close coming up and they are at Little Big Horn, at many other battles and flee to Canada together. Gall belongs to the secret Strong Heart Society, he is sponsored by Sitting Bull. This elite group of warriors had two members who stake themselves to the ground in battle and fight to the death. It is a world of motion, after all they are nomads, and yet a deep rootedness in the ground. All this is erased by the reservation life after the wars. Gall winds up a farmer, becomes fat and tries to lead his band on that impossible path between the traditional life and the new incarceration. Years after his death, his name is assigned to a railroad hamlet, one built by a line he had fought to stop during the wars. The town fails in three years, Gall's fame and memory fade.

There is a story of Gall when he was eleven years old. He is in a snowball fight and according to the rules, if you are struck, you fall dead to the ground and cannot move. Finally, he is the last boy standing on his team and he retreats to a water hole. Suddenly a gray wolf emerges. His opponents flee because they think Gall has shape-changed into a wolf. So his side wins.

At Little Bighorn, Gall witnessed the murder of women and children and found his own family missing, most likely dead. He later said he went kind of crazy. He stormed into what came to be called Custer's Last Stand wielding a hatchet, and smashed the skulls of other men more times than he could recall.

This is known because ten years after the event, he stood on the same ground with a US military officer who had survived the battle and gave his account of the combat.

It was largely an accident. The temporary campsite of the Sioux was called Greasy Grass, a place the gathered tribes planned to abandon that day, since their vast pony herds could no longer be sustained by the surrounding hills of grass.

Then, the soldiers came.

* * *

Marauders cross the land, various Indian groups drifting toward fortune. The Apaches drop down from the Great Slave Lake in Canada, the Sioux wander out from Wisconsin, the mound builders line the rivers and streams of mid-America and then vanish. Europeans come from all directions and everyone claims ground and keeps moving, stabs beasts, hits new neighbors in the head, says the earth is sacred and abandons it for new horizons.

For thousands of years, North America has had net migration and endless wanderings of the people already here.

I drive but I am never on the road, only the machine touches asphalt. I am not seeking to discover America. Sometimes I'll drive five thousand miles to a destination and want to leave as soon as I arrive. I have no purpose on the road, but I have an appetite. Part of it is night, headlights barely sketching out the ground flying past. Also, the tired faces in truck stops at midnight where I sip bad coffee for five minutes. I study the lines at the restroom when a bus stops and the homeless line up for relief. The stale pizza under heat lamps gives off a soft glow of rot.

I do not hear the song of America; I do smell the fatigue.

Two things draw me on: the blur of landscape and the flow of things in my head. I have driven a hundred miles at night with no memory of a single truck, car or highway sign.

I am in Big Cypress Swamp in Florida and there is a hummock with fruit trees that have gone wild, a place where the Seminoles hid a village during the long wars.

I see an alligator break water, flop backwards and disappear.

I move on.

Up on the Lost Coast of northern California I touch an old grove redwood while just below the breakers smash against the coast.

In Mississippi near the river, a Vietnamese sells me a carton of cigarettes in the piney woods.

A girl is pumping gas in Texas with a bare midriff rolling with fat.

I catch a sunrise in central Nevada.

The cops stare with serious eyes as I stand outside a gas station at two a.m., rub my hand on the stubble of my beard, my hair long and uncombed, my Levi's dirty and shirt wrinkled and half unbuttoned.

This can go on for days and nights.

It suits me.

I seek pumps that take debit cards so I do not have to speak to anyone.

I play no music.

I find photographs and letters about trips taken by my father in the twenties and thirties, drives by automobile from Chicago to the West Coast, or down to Florida, rides pursued when highways were ideas more than facts.

The trips have no explanation.

So I am not original.

Jude

I would hear a few stories sitting in the kitchens of old houses in northwestern Iowa in the early 1950s. The ducks and geese had once been clouds, the prairie had been unfenced and studded with potholes left by glaciers. My father saw men on Main Street wearing guns, and then I stumble upon old photographs and see that the Lake Park, Iowa, of his childhood was a handful of frail frame buildings on a muddy street, a treeless place sitting like a scab on the endless prairie.

In my father's country in northwest Iowa, the Ocheyedan mound, somewhere over 1600 feet, was felt to be a high point. As a boy I would be taken there to marvel at what looked to be a mere bump on the prairie. Early settlers assumed it was some Indian burying ground, but it is simply the relict of the main glaciers that crept over the region and in the northwest part of the state left deep deposits of loess, a rich ground for farmers.

Fred Nagg come to this blank on the prairie in the winter of 1871–72, built a sod hut and suffered through blizzards. Finally, he could bear no more, and started walking for supplies to the store miles distant. They found his body in March after a thaw, half eaten by wolves. That same winter Dr. Hall and his boy Arthur went out to cut some willows by the creek. But a blizzard came up and they headed back. The boy finally noticed that his father was missing in the whiteout. Arthur survived. Dr. Hall was found in the spring when a dog brought a human bone to a farmhouse and careful back-tracking led to the doctor's carcass.

I am staring at a photograph of my father working as a teller in the Bank at Harris, Iowa, a hamlet near Lake Park and the fabled mound. Two men stand wearing suits, two other men in overalls stare out at the camera. My father is in vest, tie, and slacks. Soon, the world war will sweep through his life.

But what strikes me is the absolute distance between his work, the bank, the faces of the men, and wolves that had barely stopped howling at the door. The country is raw, but already the tribes and the grass and the wildlife are as distant as the glaciers in the minds of the settlers. The Indians had been exiled in the years before the Civil War, with the Spirit Lake Massacre near Lake Park a small final raid, much like the Sioux raids into Minnesota in 1862.

The letter is old, the handwriting in ink so perfect it looks engraved. It is in English, no doubt due to the suppression of all things German in Iowa during World War I. It is from some friend of my mother's father writing to him from Paullina, Iowa, on December 15, 1918. They are obviously kinsmen in that easy sense of a German colony with constant intermarriage and large families. My grandfather is living in Iona, Minnesota, in the southwest corner near the Iowa line. It is a belt of Germans tilling the ground and throwing up churches to their Lutheran God.

Everyone is dying from the flu and R. B. Knuth is writing from his son's bedside.

"The epidemic," he reports, "certainly did some bad havoc here already and no one can tell when a change for the better will come. Mrs. Jos. Messner also became a victim of the dreadful sickness and was buried yesterday."

The school is closed.

"If, however," he offers, "one has the right spirit, he may celebrate at home and glorify our dear Lord by giving him praise and thanks for sending his only begotten Son in this sinful world to deliver us from the fangs of Satan."

He writes in that perfect hand as he sits by his boy's bed as the son teeters on the edge of the grave. My grandmother will be dead in a year, twenty-nine years old, two children under ten.

I am in the maze of my mother's people, tidy farms, prayers in German, small horizons and orderly lives periodically raked by plague and bankruptcy.

My grandfather has written seeking honey from Mr. Knuth, who explains, "I would not *sell* you any honey if you give me a dollar per pound but I would give you all you and your beloved family would care to eat if I only had some. Our bees were on strike last summer on account of there being no clover in the fields."

So he has sixteen hives and nothing to show for tending them. He does compliment my grandfather on his wife's skills in raising geese—"You surely can be proud of her." He is sorry the turkeys failed, "sometimes they simply die out of mere spite." For himself, he sticks to hogs.

Then comes the pitch: "Since you have such a nice home now you ought to have some kind of musical instrument." Knuth is selling player pianos because "people are getting up to date here." Already, he's sold four at $475 and his competitor in the area is charging $600 for an inferior product.

The letter trails off with more reference to the deadly flu. His boy is getting restless in the bed and he must close.

The brown leather coin purse suggests "Deposit Your Money In The Lake Park State Bank Lake Park Iowa." This advertisement is nicely embossed. Inside, I find a key and on the chain a medallion that says "I Am Insured By Travelers." Also, a lapel pin with a blue background and the flared wings of a German eagle. There is a large German coin stamped 1900 with a bas relief of the Kaiser. This is what my father's brother Charlie brought back from the war after being gassed and crossing over the Rhine.

Heartland

He lives and dies an American. Early in the nineteenth century, a boy belonging to the Omaha tribe is stolen by the Sioux. He learns their tongue, becomes a man of influence and then one of his sisters marries a French trader named Joseph La Flesche. They have a son in 1818. The wife grows weary of her trader husband's long absences and leaves him for a member of her own tribe. The six-year-old boy, also named Joseph La Flesche, visits his Sioux kin for three years, also learns the language, and then comes home to find that his biological father has returned. He tries to get his son back but the aunt refuses to give him up.

After a few years of contention, the boy is restored to his father and they go to St. Louis where he learns French. Within the Omaha tribe, the boy flourishes and becomes a favorite of Chief Big Elk. So he is this creature of many things: he knows Omaha, Dakota, Iowa, Pawnee, Oto, French, and English. He is good at the hunt. And in time, he decides he is Omaha and settles with the tribe along the Missouri. He knows the white world and knows it is coming to his ground.

When Big Elk dies, La Flesche inherits his chieftainship. He is sharp in his dealing with the US government—refusing trade goods in treaties because the agents deliver junk and cheat on the amounts, and demanding and getting payment in cash.

He plots a new world where he will build a modern village for his tribe.

The more conservative members of his tribe call this development "The Village of the 'Make-Believe' White Men."

There is a lumber mill, straight streets, regular frame houses, roads, a steamboat landing on the Missouri, a general store, plows and oxen. Strong drink is banned and drunkenness punished with the lash. He refuses to let his own children be tattooed in the tribal manner so that they can move into the greater world.

When he dies in 1888, he has created a fantasy and this is ground under by the wheels of nineteenth-century Indian policy.

There are so many make-believe white men. My mother's people tilling their fields and speaking German, my father's people insisting they are true Americans despite their disorderly and sometimes lawless ways. Joseph La Flesche trying to bring his people into a society that lacks a definition, is battered by endless waves of migration, lacks a shred of honesty in its self-description, and is relentlessly chewed up between the cogs of an industrial machine as it clings to images of farmers, woodsman and all but exterminated buffalo.

In 1913, the Indian head nickel appears and runs until 1938. On one side is a Native American, on the other side the buffalo. That is the way we survive in the make-believe white men village.

*   *   *

She is dying in slow motion, her body frail, the cigarette barely under control in her hand. She lies on the couch in the living room, a cup of weak coffee near at hand, and flicks ashes hopefully toward an ashtray but usually misses. I've seen photographs of her as a younger beauty making her way in the Los Angeles of the twenties, and she trails a dark legend of running a speakeasy on the Mississippi River. Her hair was red then, and still it has an echo of that from her journeys to a beauty shop. She is around eighty, but as her body fails her mind storms on.

Back in the mists she explains there is a Lord Cedric Bowden, and then somehow descendants came from Devonshire, England. They settle in Minnesota near a town called Preston before the Civil War.

She says these things matter-of-factly, things memorized of no particular note to her. Like her brothers and sisters, she has never been interested in family trees or the past in any guise. Richard has five children that live—Sam, my grandfather, born June 18, 1860, Ernest, George, Charles Freedman, and Nellie. And five that die during a diptheria epidemic in Jackson, Minnesota. Also, two daughters named Polly, one after another, who both die. There is a winter of deep snow, my aunt explains, and they run out of salt.

The room is a haze of smoke, her lined face catches the light coming through the windows, and she slowly exhales, coughs and then pauses in her inventory of the dead.

She knows almost nothing of Richard and his brother. James never learned to read or write, she adds, and went off to Nebraska in the sand hills around O'Neill. Richard, she says, leaves Preston, Minnesota, for the Civil War and when he comes back talks up how tough the southern boys were and how they were defeated by dysentery, not the Union army. She gives a soft laugh at this comment.

His war begins October 2, 1861, in the 3rd Minnesota Volunteer Infantry Regiment, and ends September 16, 1865, when he is mustered out. There are 901 men in the unit and when the war ends 296 are dead, all but twenty-one from disease. They fight their war with Belgian muskets, which they despise, and supplement these with private arms—Kentucky rifles, squirrel guns and shotguns.

They take riverboats down to La Crosse, Wisconsin, then

ride the rails to Chicago, getting off the train for a supper in Portage prepared by the local ladies. By July, they are in Kentucky. In a battle at Murfreesboro, they are surrounded by Confederates and surrender. Some of the men are bitter about this and later President Abraham Lincoln dismisses all the officers of the unit. In a few months, they are paroled, meaning they can go home but cannot take up arms against the rebels again.

But there is no shortage of people to kill. The Sioux rise in '62, sweep into Minnesota and kill an estimated 800. The local bishop notes in defense of the tribe that "a nation which sowed robbery would reap a harvest of blood." The 3rd, now a toothless unit insofar as fighting the south is concerned, is unleashed to take them out. They move through the tall grass and 700 Sioux fall at the hands of 270 volunteers who then retreat. But the tribesmen lose in the end and 303 are sentenced to be hanged at Mankato, Minnesota. Lincoln spares most of them, but thirty-eight swing on the ropes in a huge rectangular gallows with a big crowd watching.

Then it is time in Arkansas and finally the war ends. Richard Bowden comes home to hungry children and hard times. Sam, my grandfather, is raised by his Uncle James in Nebraska, and my aunt thinks his brother George wound up down there also.

Richard eventually homesteads in Fremont Township in eastern South Dakota. A faded photograph comes down of the failed effort—a field, a line of trees, a small wooden and empty house leaning in the wind, and behind that a tiny barn to hold the harvests that never seemed to come. He migrates to Nebraska with equal bad luck. He dies in Sioux City, Iowa, in the final years of the nineteenth century. His last act is to marry a very young girl so that she can inherit his Civil War pension.

His brother James marries a Mrs. Stewart, a rich widow, and then migrates to Cedar Rapids, Iowa. The money is lost in due time and he dies in 1933 in Portland, Oregon, living in poverty with an oil portrait of the fabled Lord Bowden.

My aunt wavers on this Lord Bowden business. She never saw the portrait and is not taken with the idea of blue blood running in her veins. She says, with some doubt, that at one point James, her grandfather's brother, offered to send her brothers Jude and Lum to England to sort out all this noble genealogy. But as she flicks some ashes I can tell she wonders at this claim.

She says as a small child she was in the Sand Hills with her dad, Sam, and the Sioux camped about in teepees. She shows a portrait of a homestead shack from her mother's people and her father is an old man sitting on a bench in front of a building that looks likely to collapse in the next breeze.

As for my aunt, she eventually fades away. She enters her eighties hosting poker games at her farmhouse that seem to go on for days and once when she has a heart attack at the table refuses to interrupt the card play and finally looks into her health a few days later.

But that afternoon, as I take notes and gently prod my aunt into the mists of a past she knows but does not treasure, she is relaxed with her smokes and coffee. She never asks what I am about, partly because my late father, her brother Jude, was considered the memory bank of the family and so she probably suspects it is part of my inheritance, this keeping tabs on ancestors.

I can hardly tell her my real motive because I can barely admit it to myself. I remember the farm, feel the spring on my face, smell the weeds and tall grass, hear the lowing of the cattle, rub my hand over the huge tractor tires feeling the big pattern designed to grip the soil, listen to birdsong, take in the shade and bumpy ground from last year's fruit under the apple trees, watch my Uncle Reddy kill a crow and hang it from the pear tree to stop their raiding.

Reddy spends some of his time, when he is not on the

river gambling, in an upstairs bedroom of the big stone farmhouse. He pisses out the window, to my mother's ire.

Her house is closed, the air stale, because my aunt feels a chill even on the warmest summer day. She speaks clearly and there is still a sting in her words, a refusal to mellow out. She is her father's daughter, and he was never an easy man.

She says her dad came to Lake Park, Iowa, in the year of the bad blizzards, 1888. He'd been living in Sioux City, the place his father had finally come to ground, and he'd run a speakeasy there because Sioux City was a dry community. But his wife, Maggie, objected to raising her kids in a saloon and went off to O'Neill in the sand hills of Nebraska to live with kin, and then after a spell to her people in Lake Park where Sam finally joined her.

"Near as I can remember," she tells me, "we lived on little legacies from mother's folks or crumbs from Uncle James's estate. Dad did some cement work on bridges, hauled freight from the station. By the time of the first war, he was basically retired and living off what his sons sent home."

Her mother's people migrated to Leadmine, Wisconsin, and a lot of them died in the mines. Her name was Margaret Ellen Hird. Her sisters were Barbara and Polly, she says, and the boys, Edward, Tom, John and James, were gangsters who spread out in Iowa and the Dakotas. Two lived in hotels all the days of their life.

I think of my father once telling me, "Don't look back there, you'll just find a bunch of horse thieves."

The past is not heroic. It was a hard country.

She suddenly smiles and tells me of Jim Rippon's brother, Gene. When I was child, Jim helped out on our farm after the war as a hired man before he prospered and descended down the hill to the steady pay of an oil refinery. During the war he'd been in the navy and escorting the convoys through the wolf packs of German submarines terrified him. He never made a secret of this fear. He knew hard times—for a spell during the Depression he worked as a hired hand for nothing more than board and keep. He was a big, handsome bruiser, and took a bride out of New Orleans, a woman from the swamps, during his time there in the navy. She'd lost a child about when I was born and so I spent my life as the half-adopted child of Jim and Nellie. And they became, according to the custom of my people, aunt and uncle though they were not blood kin.

When I was about seven, he took me to a union hall and had a beer and explained to me that if I ever crossed a picket line, he'd have to kill me.

Well, my aunt rolls on, Gene weighed about four hundred pounds and was Jim's half brother. He'd go down to the bar in Lake Park, sit on a stool and nod off for hours. One night, he fell asleep as usual but they found at closing he was actually dead.

"They had to take out a wall," she laughs, "to get his body out."

She has a deep cackle and now, at this memory, she laughs and coughs and flicks more ashes toward the ashtray as if it were a basketball shot.

Our farm, that big stone house with fourteen rooms, the two barns, the creek with fish jumping, the night crawlers fresh dug from the garden in a tin can with some wet soil, and my bamboo pole and bobber down there under the trees on the bank.

She doesn't know about the farm, how in my wanderings a few years back, I'd driven down the old road and come up the hill and parked to take a glance at the huge place. I knew the barns had been torn down by the oil company along with all the other outbuildings when they bought it as an executive country club and the fields had gone to golf. But no one had told me that they'd bulldozed the huge limestone building.

And so I never told her, or my father.

I was raised by people who'd been poor, very poor, but I never missed a meal or had to fret about having a home and clothes and schooling. I started working at age ten for money (before it had been in the fields with kinfolk), but this discipline has nothing to do with my keep and everything to do with my parents' fear that I would not know the virtue of work and the value of a dollar. So I was middle class with the values of people who knew what it meant to have nothing.

I was ripped from the farm as a home at three, and yet never left it even as my parents put all thought of it far behind and enjoyed the sidewalks and bright lights of the city.

My aunt coughs again, and then tells me she's kind of tired and we will have to do this some other time when she's rested.

But when that time came, she was in the burying ground across from her farmhouse.

As a boy, I had a coonskin cap, a cowboy outfit with two six-shooters, and that toy farm set complete with barn, tractor, manure spreader and combine. My father mocked my farm set, told me the land was a curse and farmers a bunch of complainers.

He'd say, "No matter what the weather is, they'll claim it is not quite right for crops and no matter what the prices are they'll claim they're not high enough, and to boot, they want the government to always rescue them while other people have to make a living on their own."

He'd get in arguments over this with my aunt as they sat up late playing cards in her farmhouse. Her husband, my Uncle Bill, never spoke. He was a huge man of few words and few moments of anger. He was one of a half dozen brothers who had little schooling and had tenant-farmed or pooled their wages and owned little places. They worked and harvested, took a weekend off in the fall to kill a deer, ducks also and sometimes a goose, pulled walleye from the lake and put them up for winter, and never complained about much of anything except the weather, the commodity prices and the fact that the cities would starve without them and that the city people never seemed grateful at all for their feed.

Once, I think I was seven or so and stumbling through ten acres of oak in late fall when the leaves were off the trees and brown underfoot, a red fox darted just ahead of me and disappeared so fast I had doubts that it really existed. And so I pushed on into the tangle of undergrowth, hoping against hope that I would somehow catch up and run with it through the woods.

I kept a skin complete with the head of a red fox in my room, something given to me by a kinsman, and I would nuzzle it through the long dark days of winter.

They talk of Missouri Valley, Iowa, when I am a child, a place some live, all visit and no one else seems to have heard about. The snow and blue geese come spring and fall— 400,000 of them—and feed on the bottomlands by the river. There is the wreck of the steamboat *Bertrand* that went down in April 1865 when my great-grandfather was still off at his war, and came back from the bottom to be a museum of little objects—200,000 bits of cargo—after being buried in mud for a century. It was bound for Fort Benton, Montana, with mercury in its hold to help extract gold from the mines so that Mr. Lincoln could pay for his war.

Jude

There is no diary, no journal, just some letters from the fall of '36. He writes very well, clean prose with unmistakable meaning. But he seldom writes and keeps little or nothing of what he does write.

He is born in 1896 in the northwestern corner of Iowa but even this fact is carelessly known to him. He spends at least half of his life thinking he was born in 1895 and when the correct date comes to his attention, he is indifferent. He is one of eleven children, eight of them survive into adulthood.

He has an almost photographic mind, can recite poems or passages read decades earlier. His past barely exists to him, a country that interests him not at all.

He will make mention of those men wearing guns around the turn of his century, the waterfowl clotting the sky. And then, no more. He holds Henry David Thoreau in mild contempt, camped out in his shack a mile from town and fresh pies.

His sisters tell me that as a boy of seven he began driving a wagon and hauling sand out of the pits. And then a little later he was hauling ice off the lake in winter to be cellared in sawdust against the hot days of summer in the small town. He is good with horses and like his own father in his younger days, has some moments as a jockey when he is still small. He once brings a racehorse to its wealthy buyer by riding alone three hundred miles over raw prairie. He never loses his love for horses.

These fragments float independent of each other. He never speaks of his childhood, of the small house filled with children, the lack of money because the father preferred strong drink and cards to regular employment.

There is an old photograph of him in school in the first years of the twentieth century. He looks very small as he sits at his desk. His eyes are blank and seem cautious about the things unfolding around him.

When he graduates from high school, the first-known person to have that much schooling in the family, the town lawyer has to spring for some new clothes so he can take part in the ceremony.

He and another man set the county record for stacking sheaves of wheat. Then they set the record for shocks of corn.

Sometimes, little flutters of fact would slip from his grasp. He is in the library of a rich man's home and every book he pulls from the shelf has uncut pages. He works at a farm for keep, and then the silence returns and he lifts his quart of beer and guzzles.

I know he roams the river and plays cards with his brother in the bars along the Mississippi and makes good money with his skill. But he never mentions a word of this to me, I only learn of these matters from others. I know he was a pin boy and then a pool shark. But I never learn this from his lips.

I know he had some rough-and-tumble years but I never hear of a fight, nor has he any interest in violence. I never hear him defend a violent action. I know he is the only son who never had to beat up his father. But I never hear a word of strife or conflict in his family.

I know his legal name is George W. And his brothers and sisters insist the W stands for Washington. But I never ask him, I would not know how.

No one calls him George anyway.

He is Jude.

Or, sometimes to his siblings, The Judge.

The war came and he did not volunteer. In that war, there was little time before the declaration and the draft. He is sent with a local guy who by the town's standard is legally blind. A few months later, the blind guy was dead. My father is made a master sergeant and trains southern boys in a camp in Arkansas. Three of his brothers go to the European war. Lum is in Flanders Field. Charlie gets gassed and crosses the Rhine. Reddy is in the merchant marine dodging those U-boats and hauling war supplies.

I knew all but Charlie. He dies in the insane asylum in Cherokee, Iowa, in '32. The family said it was because of the gassing. My mother insisted it was syphilis. An aunt told me they had to lock him up "after he went at Mother with a hoe."

I have a picture of Charlie and my father in uniform standing under the trees. The family is in the middle distance looking at their two boys who made it back alive.

To my knowledge, none of my uncles or my father believed in the war. They went because they had to and whatever killing they did was simply in order to stay alive. Some of them muttered that they hated the French more than the Krauts. My father always contended until the day he died that if we had stayed out of the war, Europe would have bled its way to sanity and made a settlement and avoided the second round twenty years later.

He despised nationalism, hated communism, had no kind words for fascism nor for any other forms of authority. He found Manifest Destiny an idea as silly as Christianity. He refused to fly the American flag on holidays. In his last years, he wanted to bomb Vietnam with nuclear weapons. When I told him I would not go to that war, he said, okay, tell your draft board to go take a shit in the lake.

After the war, there is nothing. Jude comes back to his small town and cannot get work. He wanders, digs ditches. The story goes silent. The next notice is from the summer of 1922 and he is in Washington, DC, where he buys a soft-leather-covered, one-volume edition of Shakespeare's complete plays, plus the sonnets. And inscribes it. He has joined the IRS and he thinks he will never be out of work again because his government will never let go of this tax.

He travels the Midwest auditing corporations. He wears good clothes. He drinks, eats prime rib at fine places in big cities. He reads constantly and tosses books away when he finishes them since he is an itinerant. He is in his twenties. His family is characterized by slow maturation and a dallying at life's various deadman's curves. He grows until his thirtieth year and his hair goes from sandy as a boy to gray around twenty to black in his late twenties. He is from Scotch-Irish and English stock on his father's side and Cornishmen on his mother's side, those hard-rock miners who arrived around Galena, Illinois, decades before the Civil War. So he comes from wastrel ways and the discipline of hard work. He goes on binges that can last weeks, misses work at the IRS, and yet is never fired because he is productive. And brilliant.

He reads classics: Gibbon's *Decline and Fall of the Roman Empire*, *Plutarch's Lives* and on and on. He learns no languages, despises all politicians, votes wet. He gets together with a brother, the one who by then lives off gambling on the river, and they chip in, retire the old man and assure their mother of permanent, safe income and tell their father to stick now to drinking and cards. The old man lives on for twenty-four years and never does a lick of work again.

But mainly he stays out of my reach. I suspect I had thousands of hours of deep conversations with my father when we would wander from coast to coast in pickup trucks and what I have scratched down is pretty much all I know of his past. He simply had no interest in his own life.

He raised me to love my country, to distrust noisy patriotism along with the antics of sports fans and other souls seeking the juice of life in packaged goods. Personal tragedies were to be felt but could not be permitted to have a larger meaning. You live, you love, you learn, you die, and let's hear no complaining. The death of a child meant more than the reports from the war. The soil underfoot had more power than the machines that pawed it into rows and crops. And in the woods all the mysteries waited and could not be explained.

My father believed in evolution but held no brief for progress. He decided after close readings that the ancient Greeks had pretty much figured everything out and since then it had just been a cascade of better data, the benefits of tinkering in the mills and ever finer machines. But no one had gotten any closer to the meaning of life, and no one was likely to get any closer because life exists and the meaning is not part of that existence.

So the material world is, but it is not enough. The feelings are real but they do not give meaning. The beginning is unknown and the ending is of no interest because for it to have interest, you must believe there is a plan and he did not believe in a plan: simply in decent behavior. And work.

I can smell an Iowa dawn right this moment, hear the crackle of thick-cut bacon sliced off a slab as it heats in the black cast-iron pan, catch the aroma of coffee coming to a boil in the pot, and the spoon whipping up the batter for the pancakes soon to be doused with syrup as gray light starts brushing against the windows. I feel the power of the Mississippi sliding through the bluffs of Wisconsin and Minnesota, hear it purring at Davenport, feel its danger at Memphis, take in the beauty on the bluff at Vicksburg, and sense some kind of brown god as it glides past New Orleans and into the bayou country and the remnants of the bird-foot delta in the Gulf.

I am ten thousand years old at least, and I am a child puzzling out my father's silences.

There is the drinking in his younger days, the card games, a host of automobiles and no savings. These details slip out on a few occasions. He enters a commercial night school, reads the law and twenty-four months later passes the Illinois Bar. He reads some books on accounting and in less than a year is a CPA in Illinois. He rents a cap and gown and sends a studio portrait to his mother and father of his non-graduation graduation. He sees Al Capone outside the courtroom where he is tried for income tax violations. He loses nothing in the bank collapse of 1933 because he has saved not a single penny from his wages.

He marries but I don't know when or why that marriage fails because he never speaks of it. My aunt told me it was because the wife was an addict, heroin or morphine, she wasn't sure. Another aunt told me they fought all the time. But basically, no one could tell me much because no one knew much because no one asked The Judge anything.

He could talk about anything because he read everything. He would argue about the tides, the law of gravity, the view of an afterlife in the ancient world, the errors of Plato, the grievous loss of the Greek paintings vanishing. He talked of things, feelings, subjects, logic, foolishness.

All of his life, he was given to vanishing for days or weeks, rambling from something and toward something though neither pole in his journeys was ever explained. I remember once spending a week sleeping in the back of a pickup on the docks at Jersey City, and each day I would take the tubes and explore New York, a marvel in my fourteen-year-old eyes, and each day he would take to the bars near the docks like a duck to water. In Washington, he got those passes for the Senate and House and took me to the gallery. At Monticello, he refused to go in because he considered Jefferson a windbag and a lying hypocrite—he believed all of the Black Sally stories decades before DNA cracked the case—and he could never forgive Jefferson for living off the sweat of slaves.

But none of these memories tell me who he was in the early 1930s when he was about thirty-five, nor what he wanted. He was propping up his siblings with regular infusions of cash, he was in the big city eating good beef, he was decked out in fine suits, had the law degree and accounting credentials, and the world he had known both economic and political was crumbling around him and he seemed indifferent. Once he told me '32 was nothing compared to the Panic of '07.

His divorced wife finally dies. I don't know the details, just a family legend whispered by his sisters, that he would never remarry while she lived.

He goes home from time to time to visit his siblings who have stayed out in the prison of the small towns. His sister Maud has gone to the West Coast, become a nurse, married and moved into another century. He decides to give her a visit but the day before he is to board the train he gets a telegram. She has had elective surgery and died on the table.

There is that trip he makes with his father, brother and sister-in-law from Iowa to the Pacific Coast. The old man wants to visit a kinsman in Oregon who is said to have a portrait of Lord Bowden. Everyone gets out of the car and goes into the house to view the portrait. Except my father. He sits outside with a cigarette. He never mentions this moment to me.

He cuts open a can and a whole chicken slides into the pan. Then dumps a can of potatoes, turns on the gas burner and applies clouds of black pepper as he nurses a quart bottle of beer. This is when she is gone and he must do the cooking. Or he is down at the barn fixing the tube on a tire while the jeep waits on a jack. He works five and a half days a week then, and his tire patching fills his weekends. That and fencing. He wears grease-stained old slacks, a white T-shirt with holes and always there is a hand-rolled cigarette burning.

He speaks to all children as if they were adults. His glasses are always being smeared with sweat and he swipes them periodically with a dirty bandana. He is the family man working to build his estate. There are two barns, hen house, hog house, the orchard, the garden, the fields. The woodlands. A domain. He speaks of never leaving, being buried in the front yard.

He hates buying anything, resents spending money. My first bicycle is secondhand and falls apart while I am riding it and spills me to the pavement. I weep with shock and shame.

I cannot understand what registers with him, what really matters.

He laughs easily and mocks everything.

Then sells the whole place—the stone house, barns, one hundred and sixty acres sliced by a creek—in a heartbeat and never tells me why.

I roll these memories around in my mind for years. I never fear him, but I never lose my anger about the selling of the farm. I live in an odd state: half in thrall to his mysteries, half at war with his behavior. Naturally, we grow very close amid our combats.

He denounces corporal punishment because he fears the violence within him. He keeps a loaded .45 close by. But he can kill nothing, not even the hundreds of chickens raised on his farm and roasted in the kitchen oven.

Sometimes strange men come to the house and then he will vanish and come home drunk. Sometimes, the drinking will go deep, last a week or more. And then he will swear off the bottles for months. He drinks beer in his light moments, Gordon's gin in his serious times. I am fascinated by the fierce head on the bottle, which to my child's eye looks like some kind of werewolf.

He has a growing bald spot and as a child I kid him about it. He'll be playing poker at the round oak table with friends, and then lean his head down so I can measure the bald spot with a tape.

He'll say, "Chuckie, tell us about riding your green snake," and then shake with mirth at my imaginary life.

In the evening, he is always reading, thick books with tiny type. None of his friends seem to read and this does not seem to bother him. He tells me stories from Plutarch's *Lives* of strange men living in some far-off time.

He despises Shakespeare's sonnets, loves the plays.

He is deadly with cards.

He does not care what people think of him. Including me.

As a child, my mother tells me, "You are just like your father."

This is not meant as praise.

He becomes for me a foreign country I can visit but never know.

There are tiny scraps of the past I learn, but they are like small crumbs falling from some locked warehouse in my father's mind. It is only when on the ground, walking a field, feeling the tassels on the green corn, ambling up a gully, sitting by a creek, smoke wreathing his face, then, sometimes, little scenes or facts fall from his lips and then he returns to his silence.

He answered to no one.

He must get out.

Bo

She is somewhere between two and three when her mother dies in 1919 in the icy heart of a Minnesota winter. The body is stacked in a shed until the spring thaws make digging a grave possible. There is an old photograph of my grandmother in her coffin in what looks like the parlor of the farmhouse. As child I once touched a watch fob made with a braid woven from her hair. Another snatch of her hair was under glass in the photograph of her corpse in the coffin.

At the funeral, someone lifted my mother up so that she could kiss the cold face of her mother, by then dead for some months.

For years, I had the story wrong. A child is working in the fields and is eight years old. The local truant officer arrives and takes the child to school. I always thought it was my mother's brother, Burnell, who figured in the story. But it was my mother, Berdina. That was the day she learned her first words of English.

There is a stepmother and she has a child with my mother's father and she does not like the two children from the earlier marriage. But mainly there is silence about those years. By age twelve, my mother is let out to work as a servant in town in a doctor's house. She becomes a motherless child. Or she ceases to be a child at all.

Fragments sometimes escape her mouth. There is a dance out there on the plains and she goes and hears Lawrence Welk and his band from neighboring North Dakota.

She rides in a wagon with an uncle at the reins. Once out of the shelterbelt of trees huddled around the farmstead, the prairie winds its course across the empty fields of November with brown cornstalks marauding across the first snow. The flat sky is slate gray and the sun hangs low in the sky without a promise of warmth. There is no money. Hard times have descended on the fields since the killing stopped in the first war. There are tractors but horses remain on many of the farms along with lean cupboards. Life is labor, the labor is hard, the returns thin. The promises of America remain distant and not really believed. Everyone speaks German in this area of Minnesota.

The wagon creaks down the dirt track with frozen ruts.

She can see her breath.

There is a present but there is not much future. Everyone goes to the Lutheran church, everyone farms, everyone puts up food, everyone struggles and nothing seems to change. There are no plans because life has been figured out right down to the Sunday service. The families rest in vast webs of kinship with cousins counting in the hundreds and families extended by blood into realms beyond accurate mapping. This is the safety net. And this is the cage no one seems capable of breaking out of. Custom dictates the days and nights. The goose is slaughtered and my mother holds the pan to catch the blood and then takes it into the kitchen so *blut zuppe*, blood soup, can grace the table. The hog is slaughtered and a child's job is to crank the meat grinder while sausage tumbles out the other end and an adult patiently twists the casing.

A January orange seems like a miracle in the faint light after the solstice.

She is maybe twelve, she can never be certain of her age when she speaks of that moment. Years later, she tossed it all out as an aside, a tiny bit of embroidery in a larger thing she wishes to draw before my eyes. Maybe it was during my newspaper days when I vanished from her eyes into a world of murder and sex crimes, stories she would never discuss with me. Only after her death did I find she had read each story and carefully pasted them all in a scrapbook.

Anyway, the uncle put his hand on her knee.

She said, "So I learned never to ride with him."

I never heard her speak of dolls or play or childhood games. Her early life was a shadowland with few or no bright memories. Her half-brother was a spoiled brat. Her full brother was overbearing. Her father was hard. Her stepmother was cruel.

After that, simply silence.

She is in nursing school. Her family tries to send her food so she can endure. She goes home during a break that fall. Her father looks out the window at an apple tree and says, "Next time you see me I may be hanging from that."

Herbert Hoover describes the current economy as a depression.

She must leave nursing school and return to her life as a servant in order to eat.

The farm is lost in the early thirties.

Her schooling is over forever.

Almost nothing comes down through time. The keepsakes of life were jettisoned in the white heat of simply trying to survive. There is an old framed photograph of my grandmother's wedding around 1910. The couple stands in front of what looks to be a new farmhouse. The building seems to have a kitchen, parlor and shed extension on the first floor and over part of the house a second story with bedrooms. It looks none too big and smells of raw lumber. In front of the house a hundred people stand, celebrants at the nuptials. There is even a brass band, no doubt a bunch of German boys from some neighboring village.

There is also the clock, a present from that wedding. It has a gold metal frame and glass panes with beveled edges on all four sides. The clock works and the pendulum swings within like a mystery. A key for winding rests on the bottom and the front opens like a door. As a child I watched that clock for hours. It was the only hint of luxury in our home and the only flash of gold in my life. It ticked loudly and so was almost never used. I connected it vaguely with my grandmother who had died twenty-six years before I was born. But mainly, I connected it with some lost portion of the earth from which my mother had come thanks to some dangerous voyage of which I knew little.

There were other fragments brought out of the lost world. Doilies crocheted by people from the same prehistory. An entire tablecloth of lace that was guarded like the Shroud of Turin and only brought out for the high holy days of family feasts. A comb or two from dead females who still mattered to the living. A tiny clutch of photographs kept in an army surplus ammunition case away from prying eyes. Two teacups, bone light, kept in a glass case and never used.

A few pieces of furniture, chests of drawers, made from walnut and retained because they were still functional. I could sense in a way they were disdained because they echoed the hard days. Just as two oil paintings of cattle grazing some Midwest pasture were hung in the darkness of the cellar. They had elaborate golden carved frames but they were never allowed into the light of life upstairs lest they seep some old poison into the new ways.

There is that old wedding photograph, the hundreds of people standing in front of the newly minted farmhouse. The future is there, a bunch of years when everyone will be whipsawed by agricultural prices, when everyone will strive to be independent and when everyone in seeking independence will grow and sell things in a market economy that functioned like a casino. In the end, almost everyone in that photograph will fail and be driven off the land and wind up in cities.

There is the chicken killing, the head on the block, the chop of the hatchet, the quick cutting and then feathers pulled with wads of newspaper wetted with hot water, that musty smell coming off the barely dead birds. My earliest memories are of chicken killing and even as a toddler I was pulling some feathers.

She raised them. And put two hundred fryers on the family table each year. No one was ever going to be hungry again.

She is terrified of the storms that roll in off the plains and this fear will never leave her. The black thunderheads get her heart to racing and the thought of a funnel cloud can all but paralyze her. I grow up loving thunder and lightning and studying the clouds for that green tone that means hail and the possibility of all hell breaking loose. I like to stand outside during heavy electrical strikes and grow excited by blinding downpours and the creeks rising, their tops suddenly a foam of racing water.

She has headaches of all types, and every month or so is struck down by a migraine. She will be in a back bedroom, the blinds pulled, the house silent. All you will hear is her rising from time to time to vomit. When the pain begins to ebb, she always tells me to fetch her two things: a 7Up with no ice and a can of peaches. Then she mends, rises, and returns to her household tasks.

The migraines always come.

The fear of storms never leaves.

There is an imagined American past and it is rooted in the soil and inhabits a country place. This Eden was the economic slave camp millions fled. I never heard my mother say she wanted to live in the country again. Not once. Not even a cabin in the woods for weekends. The ground seemed to mean no more to her than brutal labor.

Sometimes, years later, we would go back to visit her people on the edge of the plains. She would be the successful girl returning from a good life in the city. The table would be very long and crowded with people and dishes. Once, I remember two geese being roasted among other entrees. Grace would be said in German and the adults would mainly speak German. The meal would take hours what with breads and endless desserts. And then the adults were likely to stay at table as the kids escaped to the barnyard and the various beasts.

Here she was always called Berdina.

In the city, she is known as Bo.

Then we would leave and drive back to the city and nothing out there on the land was mentioned or missed by her.

She had her own hungers, and did not share them with me but I could sense them by the silences on some things and by chance remarks.

Once, when she was in her seventies and widowed, I paid for a trip to Europe with stops in various countries.

When she returned I asked her how it went.

She said, "If I wanted to be around a lot of people, I can just go to Chicago."

So she is there, trapped on the plains as the ability to find work vanishes.

She must get out.

Heartland

They are in the other room seated around the stained oak table with the dark grain. They're playing poker, small stakes because you can't clean out kinfolk. I am small, three, maybe, four, I crawl on the floor and get beneath the round oak monster without notice. They are mainly men with a few women sitting in who know the game. They all smoke, there are beers, the other women hang back so as not to interfere but still to be part of the game.

Once rolling, the game has no beginning or end and when it finally ends, and they always do, it is simply until the next hand at the table. The voices rise and fall, there is laughter and pools of silence.

I toddle out the backdoor into the farmyard as a child. There are arrowheads in the furrows, planes overhead, the thumping engines of old tractors and the cows watching with huge eyes. My father was escaping something he knew. And I was trying to find something I knew by rumor and instinct but could not name.

Before I have memory I live fantasies in the fields and meadows and woods. I invent paths and then lookouts and live my secret life. I slowly scrape trails through the leaf litter and am amazed that my feet gouge the earth and create tracks. I dream of weapons—spears, bows and arrows, guns—as things that will connect with the rabbit vanishing into the brush, the bird fleeing into the sky. Deer sometimes appear like gods in the thickets. There are hopes of elk and buffalo and mammoths in the pasture.

When older, I spend a lot of time alone walking.

I devour everything about guns, farming, animal husbandry and killing. I sneak up to second floors in old farmhouses and root out boxes of ammo, smell gun oil and feel the edge on hunting knives.

A branch cracks underfoot, a snake slithers through the grass, crows caw at me from their roost, I trip and fall, the wet earth smothers me with scent, I fear the night but love the stars.

The sticky feeling of rabbit guts on my hand, the softness of the fur still warm with heat from the murdered body in my young hands.

I am in Chicago and have just turned three.

There is confusion in the house and it is in my mind.

I sleep in a room where the window stares at the brick wall of the building next door. The passageways between the apartment buildings smell of piss, the snow is black after a few hours because of coal dust, the rag men still sing out and drive horses and wagons down the alleys, the women wear assertive brassieres and sit on stools like fat goddesses in the taverns and I am allowed in there with kinfolk and play table shuffleboard while the men drink and smoke. At night, you can hardly see a star and the women in my neighborhood if young look hunted, if old wear support hose, if older go to mass each day and live with the dead.

It is late at night and I am seven. We are wandering in a huge apartment building with Halloween bags in our hands like we are animals, vandals destroying store windows with obscene words we do not understand, throwing rocks through glass, starting fires in cans during the dark hours. We are going down a hallway in this cell of apartments, a mausoleum built in the twenties, and we knock on doors, and one opens, and the woman is probably less than twenty-five, and she has scent, red lips, hips, and breasts, and she invites us in—three boys under ten—and we hesitate, and finally say no. And I will regret that decision until the day I die.

As a boy, I pushed a yellow news cart through snow and ice in Chicago. I was nine or ten. The paper boy had been beaten by neighborhood toughs, his cart set on fire.

My father walked with me for a few days. This was my great shame, one that continues when I remember it. The gray sky, my fear, my trepidation over my first real job folding papers, pushing the cart a good mile to the route, tossing the papers onto third-story back porches.

Eventually, I pulled myself together and things worked out okay.

But years later, sitting in the dark alone in the desert and listening to the flow of cries and faint footsteps around me—one of those nights when you awaken because of some sound, then drift back to sleep and at dawn see fresh coyote tracks around where your head has lain—it all came back to me, the fear gripping my guts, that acid flavor on my tongue and my small nine-year-old body pushing the cart through snow and gutters of ice.

I remember sitting there drinking cold beer on a hot day with a friend—his wife whirling in and out of the room brimming with matronly concerns since it is ten in the morning—and the scent of a hot woman from some hours before seems to be coming off my hide. He is talking about the bandsaw he just bought and what he dreams of making with it. I'm thinking he is ahead of me because I don't have dreams. I have appetites, and I lack the skills at the moment to feed them and the words to explain them.

They start on North American ground about fifty-four million years ago, get the design of the hoof worked out about six million years ago, and vanish when ice goes out about ten thousand years ago.

They come within human reach in the steppes, that borderland of Europe and Asia, about six thousand years ago. At first we eat them, then herd some, then slip on top. Remains show wear on some ancient teeth from a bit. There are hints in abandoned human sites of bridles.

The raids start, the endless pouring of people out of the grasslands of Asia and into Europe, people riding the wild energy of horses. They come back to their old home on Columbus's second voyage. Spread slowly into the hands of Indians, put their hoofprints deep in our dreams and then slip away and become toys we keep around when we have the money.

But in that moment when a person first climbed up on a horse and rode, velocity increased 1,000 percent and life became the wind in our face. We think velocity is new, change is new, and this vast tumult and wave of fear is new. And we are wrong. There has never been firm ground for our lives and our only balm has been a forgetfulness of the changes we have endured.

My father could name every part of a horse and all the tiny pieces of harness that came out of its mouth with proper names that sounded like song when I was a boy. It was a serene moment he savored as the world exploded around him.

Delta

It is simple and so it is almost never remembered. The French settled New Orleans in 1718 in order to cork the lower Mississippi and control trade from a vast inland empire of the Ohio, the Mississippi and the Missouri Rivers. The vast tract and the city became Spanish, then French again, and following the destruction of a French army in Haiti who underestimated the lust for freedom in their black slaves, it was tossed into the lap of Thomas Jefferson in the Louisiana Purchase for three cents an acre.

Jefferson was willing to forge an alliance with Great Britain and make war to get the city. As it turned out, Napoleon, licking his wounds from the debacle in Haiti, and anxious for funds for his projected European wars, cut a deal in order to focus on his campaigns. On April 18, 1802, President Thomas Jefferson penned a note to his negotiator in France: "There is on the globe one single spot, the possessor of which is our natural and habitual enemy. It is New Orleans through which the produce of three-eighths of our territory must pass to market." The Louisiana Purchase changed the ownership. Nothing can change the reality of the essential port or the essential drainage.

That is the long and short of it: the bulk of the American West and the roar coming off the Great Plains entered the life of the United States because controlling New Orleans and the traffic spilling down the great rivers was essential for the survival and future of the young republic. To stand in the Dakotas is to stand on ground that came as a doodad affixed to the scheme of getting New Orleans. The wheat fields and the bayous are inseparable and all that came after that moment is intertwined.

In the whiskey bars of the plains people tap their feet to music that first came into being in the city near the river's mouth.

For me it has always been tied together. As a child I was whisked from the hayfields and taken downriver and into the bayous. I am a mixture of bullheads and soft-shell crabs. In my life and in my heart, the gumbo sits next to the fresh apple pie cooling on the sill. This connection forged by Jefferson is lost to memory now. But it is as vital for a wheat farm in western North Dakota as for a Cajun gliding through the bayous, hunting gators.

Here is where the avalanche of soil settled after the ice retreated and the glacial lakes of the upper Midwest headed south with a roar some thousands of years ago. The Delta blues are grounded in debris from the Dakotas and upper Midwest. And this crossroads brought more than commerce. Drums came up from the Caribbean, stringed instruments and Senegalese scales traveled downriver as Virginia slaves trudged to the death camps of Louisiana sugar plantations. The city became the warehouse of American music and in many ways of the American imagination. It is declared alien by other Americans who are spooked by its Babel of languages, race mixing and large black population.

Forty years ago I was by the levee in the Mississippi Delta at the shack of a bootlegger. She was an old woman living in the woods with a still and an elaborate set of wigs—red, blonde and so forth. We got drunk on her moonshine for an afternoon by the great river. Her skin was very dark and her laughter was very light. She shone in the afternoon sun and was like a benign gremlin as she handed around the jugs of her booze.

And then after weeks in the delta living with black people and being scorned by white people, I headed downriver and went to New Orleans and ate étouffée, had my beignets, drank the coffee with chicory and felt the velvet nights and mosquitoes. I would stand on the levee and watch the river flow, a muscular snake almost done journeying from Pittsburgh and Minnesota and the eastern flanks of the Rockies.

My aunt would ply me with food, and it was very good since she ran a restaurant in the city. And she would cluck and mutter about my living with black people and having anything to do with the great change that was sending tremors through her white world. She would force-feed me Johnny Cash from her collection in hopes of saving my white soul from the pull of coloreds and their thumping music.

Eventually, I left, drove north along the river, drifted through Memphis where my Wisconsin license plates drew angry eyes, crossed the river and went along the Arkansas Delta and then into Missouri and tasted the old French towns that once greeted Daniel Boone.

Heartland

Iowa belches forth Bix Beiderbecke and his horn and Bix goes down to the river one evening and hears a steamboat coming into the pier and there is this wonderful music pouring off the ship, sounding unlike anything he has ever heard and it is the horn of Louis Armstrong who has come up from New Orleans, or so the story goes. The percussion of the song is the snap of brassiere straps, the melody is a moan, the chorus shouts, the river whispers, the wind comes up, dust in the air, then a moon rises, and still the engine purrs down the black top and the white line, it moves, from road to table to road, it snakes across my country.

Charles Ellsworth Russell played the clarinet real well and was called Pee Wee. He was born in St. Louis, raised in Muskogee, Oklahoma, and could not get music out of his head after hearing some players from New Orleans perform at the Elks Lodge when he was a boy. He is part of the tangle that is a culture. He left for St. Louis in order to get his music down. In the summer of 1922, he was playing at the Central Café in Ciudad Juárez which had a blooming colony of people from the US who liked a drink and some heroin when the mood hit them.

He is sixteen years old and playing the saxophone in a band. At night he hires a Mexican cop for a buck to protect him as he drinks and makes his rounds. He goes to see a bulldog-badger fight, dismisses the cop, gets more drunk and lands in jail. Three days on bread and water till the band leader finds him and makes his bail. Then he spends a lot of time in the southern states and gets spirituals and the blues in his head.

Then he met Bix Beiderbecke and they made music together for years.

It's all a tangle, to my great comfort.

There is a moment in Russell's life that feels good to me. He is playing the clarinet now, his final instrument. He drinks a lot and he improvises all the time. He is doing a gig at the New England Conservatory of Music. One night, a student comes up to him and gives him some sheets of music, page after page almost clotted with notes.

Pee Wee asks, what is this?

The student says, this is your solo from last night. I transcribed.

Pee Wee says, "This can't be me. I can't play this."

The student assures him he did play it.

Pee Wee says, "Well, even if it is, I wouldn't play it again the same way—even if I could, which I can't."

He tries at times to explain what he does.

He says, "You take each solo like it was the last one you were going to play in your life. What notes to hit, and when to hit them—that's the secret. You can make a particular phrase with just one note. Maybe at the end, maybe at the beginning. It's like a little pattern. What will lead in quietly and not be too emphatic. Sometimes I jump the right chord and use what seems wrong to the next guy but I know is right for me. I usually think about four bars ahead what I am going to play. Sometimes things go wrong, and I have to scramble. If I can make it to the bridge of the tune, I know everything will be all right. I suppose it's not so obnoxious that the average musician would notice. When I play the blues, mood, frame of mind, enters into it. One day your choice of notes would be melancholy, a blue trend, a drift of blue notes. The next day your choice of notes would be more cheerful. Standard tunes are different. Some of them require a legato treatment, and others have sparks of rhythm you have to bring out. In lots of cases, your solo depends on who you're following. The guy played a great chorus, you say to yourself. How am I going to follow that? I applaud him inwardly, and it becomes a matter of silent pride. Not jealousy, mind you. A kind of competition. So I make myself a guinea pig—what the hell, I'll try something new. All this goes through your mind in a split second. You start and if it sounds good to you, you keep it up and write a little tune of your own. I get in bad habits and I'm trying to break myself of a couple right now. A little triplet thing, for one. Fast tempos are good to display your technique, but that's all. You prove you know the chords, but you don't have the time to insert those new little chords you could at slower tempos. Or if you do, they go unnoticed."

My father is seven when he is born and thirty-six when he dies. Bix Beiderbecke becomes the young man with a horn, the white boy from Davenport, Iowa, who sucks up the sounds coming from New Orleans and pours them through his Midwest cornet. He is raised in a two-story house of Victorian statement, a small porch with a turret roof beams from the second floor off his bedroom. His father's name is Bismarck and the house on the safe street is the last place people expect to hatch that young man with a horn.

By age five, he has taught himself the piano and can reproduce whatever he hears. At age seven, he makes the Davenport paper: "Little 'Bickie,'" as his parents call him, is the most unusual and the most remarkably talented child in music that there is in this city. He has never taken a music lesson and he does not know one key from another, but he can play in all completeness any selection the air or tune of which he knows. By the third grade, he has become the wild child. When scarlet fever knocks him down and keeps him out of school, his mother hires a music teacher for the boy. He refuses the rote manner of music instruction and only likes the ways he has invented. He loves the music of Debussy. He absorbs performances and repeats them letter perfect, including the mistakes. A friend notes that the boy could "tell you the pitch of a belch."

He ignores his classes and is forced to repeat one year. At the same time, Louis Armstrong is feeling frisky on North Rampart on New Year's Eve, fires that pistol and is hauled off to a juvenile facility. Where he discovers his horn.

His brother comes home from World War I with a Victrola and the "Tiger Rag." This is the first moment Bix hears jazz and he buries his head in the big horn of the machine for hours. A neighbor gives him an old dented cornet. Bix slows the speed on the Victrola and spends hours mastering the notes. This goes on for weeks, the house shaking from short blasts of his horn—a misery resolved by getting him a mute. Then suddenly, he is letter perfect. He has his own technique, one that uses the third valve a lot, one hardly touched by most horn players. In high school, he sings in a quintet, the Black Jazz Babies. He cannot read music but what he hears comes out of his horn. He's a bust at high school and gets in trouble for allegedly messing around with a five-year-old girl. He's shipped to an academy on the fringes of Chicago and fails there also. He becomes a student of the speakeasies where the new music is played.

He is in and out of bands. He still can't read music and his appetite for solos grates on band leaders. But he meets Hoagy Carmichael, an Indiana boy also isolated by the music fluttering in his head. Beiderbecke is the guy who can improvise.

Dakotah

The ground scares people with its illusion of endless horizon. And this fear leads to a fantasy, that the plains are flat. Only 5 percent qualify for pancake status, the rest is rolling land. The absence of trees except along streams instills a mild panic in people and the plains induce a frenzy to get across them and reach the embrace of forests or mountains.

There is the matter of the wind. There are the blizzards. Always drought hangs over the land like a thought. Houses huddle in the draws or in the wind breaks made by planting trees, and when the hill is topped and the small town finally comes into view it has the feel of a harbor on a vast sea. Various names have been fixed to this ground including the Great American Desert, which came out of the recurring dread from an early military expedition. After that, it was at various times hailed as the new Garden of Eden.

Nothing has ever been easy here. The cities to this day sit on the edge of the plains and stare into it with anxious eyes. As a boy I was spooked by kinsmen from the plains with their tales of farmers frozen by whiteouts during simple walks to their barns, of children who vanished into drifts on their way home from classes, of cows dead as posts in the Siberian air, cars smothered by blizzards and the occupants killed. There was a potential immigrant to Kansas in the late nineteenth century who on his first visit was frozen to death with a booster pamphlet in his pocket comparing the local climate to that of Italy.

Frank L. Baum came to the Dakotas in the late 1880s, was crushed in three years and retreated back to the Midwest where he invented Oz, a girl named Dorothy and laid down the first American fairy tale of a place where life is hard, the land is murderous and you hope a wizard can make things right.

Daniel Boone

It is October 1744 in Pennsylvania and Squire Boone buys twenty-five acres of woods and pasture five miles from home. His ten-year-old son Daniel and wife Sarah summer there with cattle and sheep and make butter and cheese. The boy roams the woods. These summers lived in Boone's mind until he finally died in his eighties.

Later, Boone becomes the hunter, the man who barely tills ground and flees into the woods. One witness to this breed of wayward American males wrote of the urge to hunt in the cool days of fall, "I have often seen them get up early in the morning at this season, walk hastily out, look anxiously to the woods, and snuff the autumnal winds with the highest rapture."

When Boone was in his teens, he made his first long hunt in the mountains with his friend Henry Miller. Afterwards, they took their hides and furs to Philadelphia and squandered all the money on a three-week spree, one that left Miller repentant over the wasted income. Boone was not repentant. Many years later, Miller told his son, "Boone was very profligate, he would spend all his earnings and never made an effort to accumulate."

On the Upper Yadkin in North Carolina Boone takes ninety-nine bears off one branch in a season. There is the tale that he and a friend once took down thirty deer in a day. Soon after settlement, the game beat it out of the country. Within a month of founding Boonesborough, Kentucky, the hunters had to range widely because all the game had been slaughtered near the infant settlement.

Disney

As a boy he catches an owl and in the ensuing struggle, he hurls the bird to the ground and kills it. Later, this incident causes nightmares. His name is Walt Disney and he is growing up in Marcelline, Missouri, fated to become the planet's Main Street when he finally fixes the world and creates his fantasyland.

Decades later, as the planet slides into another world war, Walt Disney struggles to conceive an opening for a new feature called *Bambi*. He can't seem to understand how to tell a story from the point of view of animals, a story in which humans—"Man in forest"—appear as killers on the hunt. Are they people pretending to be animals or what? Suddenly at a meeting with his animators he announces an inspiration, "just the flash that came to my mind here," and then he is off like a raving preacher and words and images spew out and he offers, "Say we open with morning in the forest. Everything is getting up. And then you come to the old Owl and he's going to sleep. And then we introduce the Squirrel and the Chipmunk. We introduce all the characters we want to in that morning . . . this noise breaks loose that's here—it's happened—where they begin flying around and the whole damned woods begins to fuss and swarm."

Bambi is born, the dead owl revives, the world will be made right.

But this world proves unacceptable. The movie is made

for a world at peace but seems to take forever and finally comes out in the flames of August 1942. It cost far more than planned, and there is little or no hope of earning back the costs. The drunken composer of the music—Frank Churchill, who had also scored *Snow White*—kills himself with a shotgun that May. A major hunting magazine revolts when hunters slaughter Bambi's mother. Disney's own daughter attacks him for killing off the mom. Later Walt Disney says, "Life is composed of lights and shadows, and we would be untruthful, insincere, and saccharine if we tried to pretend there were no shadows."

The scenes for the killing ground pour straight out of Walt Disney's mind. He has mainly kept away from *Bambi*, been buried in *Fantasia*, *Dumbo* and *Pinocchio* and in keeping his studio alive as it slides toward financial ruin because of his own craving for perfection and total control of his imaginary world called Walt Disney Productions. It takes over a thousand employees to create what people see on the screen but they remain all but anonymous and his name is on everything. Some question what exactly Walt Disney even does as he flits from one meeting to another and one project to another. He can't even draw.

It is June 1941 and *Bambi* has been underway for four years. There is one problem: how to put up on the screen the moment human beings murder Bambi's mom. Do bullets puncture her body? Does Bambi witness the gore?

Walt Disney takes a meeting on the problem and suddenly blurts out, "He's hunting for his mother, and he never finds her, and the Stag just tells him. . . . He sort of wanders around. The last you see of them is just some faint silhouette forms back of this blizzard and pretty soon they have disappeared and there is nothing but snow falling."

The scene becomes the emotional touchstone of the movie, the frames where death brushes against the American matinee world.

My Piece of Ground

My first guts are fish. The blade makes the cleaning vital to me. I am fascinated by knives as a child and spend hours sharpening blades on a stone, then shaving hair from my arm to certify the edge. Slicing the fish open, reaching in and ripping out the slimy guts. That is the beginning. I dream of fish, at one point bring a bullhead back from a pond and keep it in a bucket in the Chicago basement until it dies after a day or two.

My parents are remarkably tolerant of my lust for other life forms. I did not expect this. My father disdained hunting and fishing and my mother resisted the mess of things. But somehow I was allowed a hamster, goldfish, small turtles in a bowl. And a rod and reel, tackle box, and rifle. All this before I was ten.

I read nothing but books about animals and dream of moose. I am not allowed a dog because my mother and father are country people and think it cruel to keep a dog in the city. I send in coupons to dog supply companies and spend hours reading of various medicines and foods and research breeds. For a brief spell, there was hope that I would feed this hunger with Cub Scouts. But I loathed the uniform, and hated the meetings.

I am in the woods of fall, scrub oak and jack pine, Wisconsin ground, my kinfolks ground, a river running through and little ponds nestled in the forest. I sprawl in a clearing, the sun warming my face, and out of the corner of my eye see a fox darting into a thicket.

Sometimes in the cold and dark of January I open my tackle box and do nothing but examine my lures, dream of a muskie taking my red and white Dare Devil spoon.

I become crazed with traps, and for a spell set up a line amid the huge oaks of an uncle's land. I catch nothing but still the spring of the trap, the act of setting it up, driving a pin into the ground, the smell of the fall, is a drug to me.

I slip across a line, cease to believe in God, hate going to church, cannot fathom the glimpses of biology and science offered up in my elementary school and create my own natural world.

It has very few rules.

There is no line between animals and humans and plants and animals and dirt and sky. The sun simply rises and sets. I try to learn all the constellations but this is difficult in a city where even the moon is barely visible.

I collect rocks.

Read hunting books.

Someone tips me to the existence of the government printing office and I order booklets on raising pigeons. My eight-year-old dream is to build a coop on the roof of the apartment building and spend my time in the open air tending my birds, and serving up fine squab at table. But this is not permitted. I negotiate a tiny patch of dirt behind the building and plant lima beans.

Jude and Bo

There are two packets of letters, hers are tied with pink ribbon, his with string. Together they number maybe 150, almost all mailed between September 1, 1936, and mid-December. When my mother died in her eighty-eighth year the letters came back. For over three years, I refused to look at them.

I finally opened them when I thought that just maybe they might help me understand my hunger for ground. I knew the letters would detail their courtship, but that did not interest me. I had experienced the pain of their marriage and yet even as a child could feel the white heat of their passion for each other. When I was five or six, my father would return each day from his work in the Loop and then immediately take a nap. With my mother. I can remember standing in the bedroom doorway wearing my six-shooters. They are both in bed under the covers, speaking softly to me, and telling me to close the door on my way out.

Jude's been out to see his folks in Lake Park and his brothers and sisters scattered about the area. It is early August 1936. Bo is tending to the house of his brother-in-law, Dr. Basil Stevenson of Fulda, Minnesota. She also works long hours at the drugstore in the town of fifteen hundred, a community embedded in the fields of southwest Minnesota. Bo's letter is humdrum—a drive down to Lake Park, a few hamburgers, winning $1.70 from a punchboard in a saloon, and Jude's invitation to come visit him in Chicago, a sixteen-hour train ride. She notes her vacation starts on the sixteenth of the month, and signs the letter Love, Bo. She's going to visit him with his sister Lucille in tow.

There is a short note on the twelfth of the month from the drugstore—"This will have to be short and snappy, I'm writing on company time"—where she's working as a soda jerk. She's won $40 at bank night at the movie theater, and she's living it up. The night before eight of them cooked up a storm and ate six chickens. Then, in four days, she is off for the big city.

She's twenty-one, he's forty-one. He is divorced. She has never had her own home, nothing more than a room in some-one's house where she cleans, cooks and washes. He is wear-ing hundred-dollar hats, two-hundred-dollar overcoats, liv-ing in a good hotel near the University of Chicago and he has that rare thing for 1936, a steady federal check. President Franklin Roosevelt will accept the Democratic nomination for a second term that month. A civil war rages in Spain, the great poet Federico García Lorca is murdered by Franco's killers. None of this has anything to do with their lives. They move in a slipstream that avoids history.

Jude is political, obsessed with Roosevelt and convinced he will destroy the world of work, merit and failure. He is the former poor boy who thinks no one really needs government help. She has not a thought on the matter—this will be the first time she'll be old enough to vote.

What she thinks is simple: on August 31 she is back from Chicago and begins her first letter "Dearest Jude."

She's been down to a family reunion of her people, she tells him, and the car was almost struck by lightning. She's run over a snake, eaten a beefsteak, and now done all the washing for the family Stevenson.

And also, she writes, "You say the day of the races and the trip to the candy store was the happiest you ever had? My feelings are mutual in that Jude.... The doctor is in a quandary—How can he give the bride away and be best man too?"

They're going to be married. His sister Lucille has been the matchmaker, the same woman who as she lay dying recited the shards of family history to me. So they refer to her as Cupie for cupid. They barely know each other. As the months roll on, they will gently inquire of each other about snoring. There will be little references to the candy store, a bar my father liked to visit. But they agree on two things: they are getting married and they are fleeing the city forever and going to live in the country.

They have already named this retreat: Rest Haven.

The trip back to Fulda had been by car. Somehow Lucille and Bo had arranged to ride with kin. The route took them through Davenport, Iowa, an old town on the Mississippi and Jude pounces on this fact in his reply—"I am tickled to death that the country around Davenport appeals to you ... And you think that the country around there is OK for raising chickens and turkeys—how about a family? It is a German neighborhood. That's proof enough that it is OK isn't it?"

He echoes again the joys of the candy store and what a good time they had and "there are going to be oodles more of them."

Two days later, he writes again. He wants a photograph of her. And he notes that "your remarks about money matters were just like you—kind, fair and generous. Thanks a lot Honey. I wasn't worrying. It only confirmed what I already knew—that you are one sweet girl."

Money is hardly an idle matter for either of them. He has it and dreads being without it ever again. She has lived a life of string saving, a habit she will never give up. In her letters, she is always tired. Doing the wash before dawn, sometimes putting in ten or twelve hours at the drugstore, then back to her servant chores. But she tells him she has just read a very good article on raising turkeys in the new *Reader's Digest*. He writes back, "Dream on, that is what makes life worth while, skip a few of the realities and dream rosy dreams of the future. That is what I am doing now. Some of them come true—ours will Bo—I am sure of it. We'll not only plan it that way but we will do it that way, won't we?"

He is working in an office with 250 other civil servants, a new boss is about to arrive and everyone is nervous. He hates his job and clings to his check. He dreams of a place called Rest Haven. They keep fiddling with a possible wedding date. She likes the idea of Christmas but he has only five days vacation left in the year, but starting January 1st he has three weeks coming and so, how about starting the New Year with a marriage? He writes of this notion in the evening as he sits alone in his hotel room listening to Alf Landon give a campaign speech that denounces the New Deal. He's spent that Sunday afternoon in the hotel lobby working crossword puzzles with other lonely men.

He wonders if she might be able to just catch a night train to Chicago for a holiday?

The farm keeps coming into his mind even as he frets over the New Deal.

He thinks, "We'll turn the rascals out yet. We want to get rid of them before we go farming so that we can raise what we want to. 'We want to be Lord of our acres.' We want lots of acres, but no aches."

There's stuff about movies—he's just seen *Showboat*, she's been to *Anthony Adverse*, there's reports of the weather, he's retired his straw boater until next spring. The farm keeps coming back, some place where they will be free. His father has sharecropped but never owned ground. Her childhood was as a slave in the fields.

"Funny thing," he decides, "this love business, isn't it? I have read and I believe 'take love out of the world and there is nothing left worth living for.'"

She says, "By the way, we don't want a large wedding? What do you think? . . . And where do I want to go? With you of course! By the way, I love you."

She is sorting out the wedding plan. Why not skip getting married in Lake Park or Fulda? If she comes to Chicago right after Christmas (she must work at the drugstore until Christmas Eve, she explains) then they would save a week of his vacation and that summer "we have to look for Rest Haven."

He agrees to whatever wedding plans she wants. "And don't think I have forgotten Rest Haven. Just as sure as fate we will be out scouting around for it next summer. In fact you and Rest Haven have a monopoly on my thoughts. I surely think of you oodles of times a day. And the thoughts are all pleasant with you and Rest Haven to look forward to."

Ah, she responds, "Landon has to win, 'cause we have to have him in order that Rest Haven pans out as planned."

The weeks creep past. She is working those twelve-hour days at the store, plus all the hours as help in the house. He's busy at the office and lonely the rest of the time. His mother is failing. His sister needs a coat—so he has a woman sew up one. The presidential election rages inside him. She has three cavities filled. The wedding date keeps shifting from Christmas to New Year's and back again. They tell each other that their love will never end.

And "Honey, your remarks about Rest Haven make me very happy. Don't ever think that it is just a pipedream of mine. I was never more sincere in my life and while I of course can't be certain that it will materialize, in my own mind I am about as sure as it is possible to be sure of anything."

He is playing the stock market and in his head he converts each day's gains into how many acres that would buy—that very day he'd earned three acres. He tells her, "We will work and we will save for the farm that we crave."

He copies out a passage from Robert Ingersoll, the great agnostic of the nineteenth century. The piece is entitled "Home," and it begins, "In the country is the idea of home. There you see the rising and setting sun; you become acquainted with the stars and clouds. The constellations are your friends. You hear the rain on the roof and listen to the rhythmic sighing of the winds. You are thrilled by the resurrection called Spring, touched and saddened by Autumn, the grace and poetry of death. . . . In the country you preserve your identity—your personality. There you are an aggregation of atoms, but in the city you are only an atom of an aggregation."

Bo

She carries herself well, a tall woman who never stoops. Her face is warm, the eyes blue and she is constantly doing something—the wash, baking bread, supervising her children, sewing, cleaning, walking to the market, killing chickens, working the garden.

I can barely remember her saying a bad word about anyone.

I never obey her and at times, this fact drives her to anger.

She never stopped working until a stroke felled her at age eighty-six, ending her three part-time jobs in a knit shop, a grocery and a crisis nursery.

She recoiled from any bad talk or cruelty and still shuddered a half century later at the memory of her father castrating a farm dog for being, in his eyes, not obedient enough.

She says to me, "I should wash your mouth out with soap."

She says to me, "You have to understand. Your father means well."

Once, I remember a drive with her. I may have been three, certainly no more than four. We slide down 79th Street in Chicago, the schools, shops, busy sidewalks flashing past my eyes pressed against the window, the scent of dust of the old prewar car, some relic from the thirties the old man had bought for a song and would run to death.

She parks, leads me down a passage between two apartment buildings, the back porches and stairs all painted the uniform Chicago gray. She knocks on the kitchen door, it opens, a man invites her in, I am told to remain on the porch.

It takes a while, the sky I recall is overcast.

Then she comes out and we leave.

Decades later, this memory floats up again.

And I think, maybe my mother was having an affair.

Dakotah

Blackbird catches a wave. In 1800, the smallpox comes and takes him away. The same disease rakes the plains between 1778 and 1783, then again in 1800–1803, in 1836–1840. Other visitors also take a toll—the influenza in 1798–1799, that whooping cough in 1818, 1820, the cholera in 1832–1834. But Blackbird is the great man, the chief who presides over a trade nexus where the Omahas do business with the French, Spanish, British and Americans and then peddle the goods to other tribes out on the plains or upriver on the Missouri. They master the horse by 1770 and for a time they are a force on the plains.

He is said to conjure up vast powers that dominate his tribesmen. Or he is said to possess a good supply of poison with which he liberally doses opponents. They bury him on a bluff sitting on his horse and this bump on the horizon becomes a landmark for river travelers. Lewis and Clark traipse up to visit the famous dead man on his mount.

But he leaves behind his people and the smallpox makes them ugly, takes many lives and breaks their will. They decide on group suicide and so they go to war against all enemies until death shows them mercy. They attack the Cheyenne, the Pawnee, the Otos but they keep surviving both the battles and the smallpox. And so they decide to live a little longer in this place by the river.

Daniel Boone

After Boone's father dies, he comes to him in dreams and Boone learns to pay heed to these visitations. If his father smiles, things go well for Boone. If he is angry, bad things happen to Boone, like an Indian attack.

He is a haunted man and so he dreams and yet sometimes dreads the dream.

In those hours before dawn on December 22, 1769, Boone's father comes toward him in a dream. Boone extends his hand but his father pushes him away. That afternoon, he is captured by Shawnee.

Daniel Boone and his brother Squire move camp often in 1770. After capturing him, the Shawnee have warned Boone not to be found again fur trapping in Kentucky. So the Boones have small fires with dry wood, live in caves, make little sound and shift constantly from place to place.

Squire heads back over the mountains with the furs for the markets of North Carolina. Daniel Boone stays. He finds an old Indian in the forest, a man left behind to die. He gives him venison.

Winter comes and it is 1770.

Captain Caspar Mansker hears an alarming sound, one he cannot quite place, in the forests of Kentucky. He moves carefully toward the disturbance.

He sees a bareheaded man alone, sprawled on the ground. And singing.

It is Daniel Boone.

Dakotah

I am down by the river and I look up at Fort Union. The chill of fall runs through the air and riffles the falling leaves on the cottonwood. Smoke curls from the chimney of the trader's house inside the palisade. The men working at the fur post, which was in its prime from 1830 into the 1850s, devoured 500 to 600 buffalo a year, but the head trader, Edwin Denig, noted that this never made a dent in the great herds they passed in their migrations.

Just below me the Yellowstone comes in and paddlefish cling to the bottom, sucking plankton. The glaciers left eight to ten thousand years ago, then the bands moved into the fresh, exposed ground and for a long time we know nothing and they seem to have known everything. Eight or ten thousand years of people camping and dreaming and we have barely a few ancient sites with stones showing telltale marks.

I walk up the hill to the outpost, a factory that functionally gutted the Upper Missouri of hides with Indians as the labor force. The beaver trade went fast, roughly from 1820 to 1835. The business of buffalo robes lasted until after the Civil War.

Everything about the plains is movement—clouds, buffalo, people. Even the tribes that settle on the river find the wild Missouri rips apart their cornfields from time to time, swallows the soils and sends them downriver, and then the village—round earthen lodges, palisades, a place with the feel of solid living—is abandoned.

A breeze floats down the river by Fort Union, a light rain falls, the current is swift and I look for my place in the commotion.

In 1834–1835, this harvest came through Fort Union: 1,970 packs of buffalo robes, 4,100 pounds of beaver, 4,000 fox skins, 9,000 muskrats.

On April 20, 1882, according to the paper in Grafton, North Dakota, a toehold on the plains felt like this: a house, $75–$150; a stable, $40–$75; a yoke of oxen, $100–$180; a team of horses, $200–$350; a plow, $21–$24; a harrow, 15–$20; chains, harness, tools, etc., $35–$50; a good serviceable wagon, $70.

Or it is 1884 and the Northern Pacific Railroad, in order to get farmers for the line, is advertising land in 200 US and Canadian papers, 68 German-language and 32 Scandinavian-language papers in the US. Also, there were 831 agents in the British Isles, and others in Norway, Sweden, Denmark, Holland, Switzerland and Germany.

Or it is the 1920s and '30s, and Eric Sevareid is growing up in Velva, North Dakota. He says of the effort to make a living on the plains, "There were days when a buggy would drive up to our house after supper and my father and a wheat farmer would sit on the porch talking in low tones, with long periods of silence, until after we children fell asleep upstairs. Wheat was our solace and our challenge. My mother, who came from a green and pleasant city in the distant, mystical East—in Iowa—feared and hated it. My father simply met the challenge without emotion, as a man should, and grappled with it as well as a man knows how. In the end, he lost. It ruined him."

Lewis and Clark

The river goes to ice, blowing snow blurs the eye, the nights have no end, the days barely stay light. During earlier storms, the buffalo stream off the plains and down to shelter in the groves along the river. Then, the men face the subzero temperatures, the air hanging like Jello, and for a few joyous days comes the killing, hot blood and raw liver knifing the endless shroud of winter. The breakup arrives, crossing buffalo are suddenly stranded on floes in the Missouri. Natives leap from ice cake to ice cake, hop-scotching until they reach a beast stranded on a bobbing slab in the river. The buffalo moves not at all, the black eyes stare and the bow or lance erases life.

Captain William Clark scratches out a record of the spectacle, the quill held between numb fingers, the ink barely liquid, and he marvels at the nimbleness of the hunters, the silence of the frozen air, the stillness of the beasts as blood flows from their wounds. He's not easily stunned—he'd once found the fresh bone of a man when he wandered the woods of Kentucky as a fourteen-year-old.

The buffalo still as a statue in mid-river on the ice, the hunter advancing with death in his eyes.

Dakotah

The temperature hangs at one above zero. The wind is down, only slight drifts whisper across the roads. The house sits as a small tomb of silver wood, two floors, small rooms, a few trees slowly dying in a grassland where they never belonged. Joe Njos homesteads the land, builds the house, then goes back to Norway for a wife. She was very attractive, maybe the best-looking woman in the area. That was in '15, or '16.

"They had one son, and one daughter," Melvin Wisdahl remembers. He's past eighty and still he can see the beauty of her face in the blank of the plains. "She kept it spotless. She always dressed like a queen. One of his nephews always claimed his uncle got her out of a whorehouse in Norway. They died after World War II.

"Then the son lived there and he was a drunkard and he lost the land. I remember the day of the auction sale, he sat there drunk and cried.

"He married some woman who came through—someone who was making the rounds. Then she took off. He died in the fifties from something. The house has been empty a long time."

Soon the house will not be part of memory. The roof will go and fall into the cellar. The walls will tilt. No one living will remember who once lived there, the woman who dressed like a queen in her tiny castle. The earth waits for the slow rot of this intrusion called settlement.

Nearby is the Bone Trail, the track the settlers used to haul the skeletal remains of buffalo to the railroad for a few stray bucks to get them through the angry winters.

The dry wind, something must be said about this wind that lashes hour after hour, a force of dust and dry eyes. Scent fills the mind and beckons, the smell of soap and labor on the clean kitchen floor, the raw dirt of the garden and the scent coming off the leaves, the cakes baking, manure piled by the barns, the breath of life itself coming off the clothes on the line, the endless hope of each first day of spring, the tug at the heart as the geese honk overhead in V formation heading south in fall and people are trapped by the long nights until the earth tilts and warmth begins to slowly lick their faces.

I once had an uncle who struggled out there during the dry days of the thirties. The time when skies were black with dust and the land left and went all the way to the Atlantic Ocean. He finally walked off, left a woman and children, enlisted in the service and then a big war came and he was sealed inside a tin can for years, a tank man in General Patton's army. Afterwards, he settled in Chicago, worked as a janitor, played the accordion at times, had himself a life. I don't think he ever went back. I never heard him mention the place.

They took me out there as a child, little more than a toddler, and they'd gather in the kitchens over the weak coffee they drank morning, noon and night and talk but the talk was soft, almost whispers, and I'd wander out in the yards and wonder where the trees went, those green towers that were everywhere further east. I would stand by the windbreaks and stare into the endless roll of brown, a space too big for the word space.

Daniel Boone

Daniel Boone and his brother Squire finally head over the mountains toward the settlements, their horses burdened with hides stolen from the Indian hunting ground called Kentucky. They pause and camp so that they can hunt some meat. Squire stumbles on a starving man in the woods. His name is Alexander Neeley. He became separated from his party, ran out of powder and slowly began to die of hunger.

But a dog found him in the woods and he befriended that dog, cut its throat, made a fire, fashioned the hide into a bag and walked on. He ate for days in the Boones' camp and then, restored, went back into the woods.

Heartland

When I was a boy in Chicago, the Great Depression still lingered in the air and crushed dreams. The commercial avenues had the look of broken teeth with vacant lots testifying to when the boom ended in 1929 and the great fear came down. Men colonized these lots like Mexican campesinos. They staked out gardens and clumps of tomatoes, rows of corn, pole beans and squash yearned in the coal sooty air of the city. Come evening, after work, the men would be out tending their gardens, a can of beer in hand. Mainly, they were Italians.

I remember a friend asking one old Italian how he grew such wondrous tomatoes.

He said, "I piss on them."

I was issued a single-shot .22 at age seven and my blood lust rose. Rabbits fell each evening as I prowled the plowed ground. Pigeons tumbled off the roof of the barn.

I was raised with thrift. My clothes were hand-me-downs, restaurants were a foreign country seldom visited. The old man shaved with a Rolls Razor, a British contraption. The metal box contained a rust-colored strop and the blade was methodically sharpened before use. Every once in a while, the blade was honed on the metal surface of the box.

As a boy I would stand in the bathroom fascinated by his sharpening of the blade and I inhaled the scent of his shaving soap that he worked to froth with a brush in a cup and then lathered on his face.

He scorned all modern devices and considered the safety razor with its disposable blades a sign of the decline of all that was good and true.

He bought and wore army surplus. He haunted thieves markets and secondhand stores.

I grew in the shadow of hard times.

I heard scraps of conversation as the men sat around the table playing poker.

The old man once said he and a brother went to New Orleans after the first great war and they swam in Lake Pontchartrain.

Jude and Bo: Two

He joins 25,000 people in a crowd to celebrate the Constitution. He is one of 30,000 to hear Alf Landon. He lives in a decent residential hotel and all the other white-collar men agree with him that Roosevelt will be defeated.

Wooing a woman half his age remains his focus. His career seems a temporary inconvenience. Once, he'd toiled at night to pass the Illinois bar, to get his CPA. He was going places, an Iowa senator had him tapped to be his key aide. He would move to Washington, DC, and wander the corridors of power.

None of this is ever explained to me. He is in Chicago, living high, going through a dozen new cars in a few years—he just kept trading them in once the shine seemed to come off them.

In my life, I never heard my father brag about anything he did. He mocks himself. He is fat, and wearing a dirty T-shirt, his hand holds a quart of beer. He peels off his shoes and insists his feet are so perfect he could have done modeling with them. He says all this in a serious voice as he constructs a burlesque of himself.

When he finally retires from the IRS at sixty, on the very earliest date possible, he ceases wearing suits and ties and I can only remember one or two later occasions when he put them on again. His fine leather shoes grow dusty in the closet and now he favors army surplus canvas models. He never works again, save at playing the market and even that hardly interests him.

His life in the cities remains largely a blank. He is in a bank in 1917 clerking, he is in DC in 1922 beginning to work with the IRS. Random photos have him in various places, always dressed formally.

In the letters during the fall and early winter of 1936, he is the man living alone, listening to a radio to kill time, dreading the dinner hour when he must go to a café and eat in solitude. Then he returns to his room and writes love letters and in these letters, he will find a farm, and leave Chicago. Maybe Davenport, Iowa. Maybe somewhere else. He will be a farmer, work that has for two generations broken everyone in his family who tried the great casino of crops and debts and small-town banks with notes always looming.

I flip through the old love letters, skip the refrains of love, barely note the little details of life—an aunt gets a temporary job tending to a dying woman, an uncle has his Dodge break down, another uncle and aunt go off into the country to pick corn and make a little money. Everyone seems barely hanging on except my father and he is living on another planet, in a nice hotel with nice clothes and all he can eat whenever he wants to stroll a block or two in Hyde Park. He sends money and clothes home but he is a city man who keeps writing about becoming a farmer.

She also is silent about her past. Her stepmother is mean to her. Her father cries too easily and cannot help her. Her brother can be overbearing. Her people are a net of kin and poverty she seems to be politely fleeing. She likes movies. She makes it to some dances. But her life is and always has been work. Then will come a bright moment—"sixty-two days until Christmas"—their target wedding day. He writes back, "We may never write another letter to each other, we won't need to write letters at Rest Haven. I trust we can live a lifetime hardly out of each other's sight."

When she gets to Chicago and they marry, he suggests she try this as a pastime: doing nothing.

He asks if she knows how to knit.

He dreams of coming back from work to a home-cooked meal.

But he never voices a single idea about her earning money. They will have a family, they will soon leave the city for the farm. And all those stars you can see at night.

He marvels at her long hours and explains that he is off work by 3:45 p.m. and only has to put in a half day Saturday.

The drugstore in Fulda where she works is owned by a friend of Dr. Stevenson, and later a son, Harold, takes over. It is a simple world where you die in the same place and station in which you were born. Harold's wife finally passes in 2005 at age ninety-eight and is remembered for cooking, sewing, quilting and playing bridge. Fulda is the kind of town flogged by Sinclair Lewis in *Main Street*. It begins as a German colony named after a village in Hesse and attracts some Swedes and Norwegians also. After her trip to Chicago, Bo refers to the place as a burg.

He continues to worry that Roosevelt's reelection will bar him from having his farm. His stocks are up, he can almost feel his escape from the IRS is within reach. And when Roosevelt wins by a landslide, it means nothing more than a hangover. His mother tells Bo, "I'm sure Jude is wearing an ice bag today."

The farm lives on like a fever dream.

It tumbles on with minor upsets. She hears Lawrence Welk and his band when they come to Fulda. Jude gets terribly upset when he imagines she is having second thoughts. He outlines all the money he has stacked—$15,000 with his bachelor brother, Reddy—and how this makes Rest Haven a certainty. Reddy has always been in the picture as a kind of sometime resident at Rest Haven, in between his gambling tours of the Mississippi River.

"It won't be long now! And Bo, I love you and you alone and will never love anyone else or want to."

They marry on December 27, 1936. My father has bribed a clerk in city hall for the papers since my mother is delayed by work and storms and arrives late.

When I am a child, she tells me she insisted he find a Lutheran minister after the civil ceremony so that she is properly married.

She tells me that she never would have married him if she knew how much he drank.

He tells his sister, Lucille, the cupid in their relationship, that he knew on his wedding day he'd made a mistake but he lacked the courage to back out.

This last my aunt tells me decades later when she is dying, coughing, smoking and making a last visit to the past.

Neither Bo nor Jude ever mentioned the name Rest Haven to me, nor did I ever hear of such a thing until I untied the packets of love letters and began to read into the night.

Dakotah

Her heart fails her and so she dies at thirty-nine and is buried on the plains. Selma Anderson Egstrom leaves seven children, one a four-year-old named Norma. It is summertime and the air is hot and sweet in Jamestown, North Dakota. The funeral is held at home and someone lifts up little Norma so she can gaze upon her mother's face for the last time.

Years later she remembers writing a lyric to the song "Melody of Love" when her mother died. She walks around the house singing, "Momma's gone to dreamland on the train."

Her dad's a railroad man prone to drink and when he is a little tipsy, he entertains with a soft-shoe routine in the post office, or breaks into song at odd hours. Things go hard with young Norma. Six months after her mother's death the family home burns down. For a spell, the four-year-old is farmed out to another family. They have a player piano and the child is mesmerized by it.

A year after her mother's death, her father remarries. The stepmother has no smiles, has a wide mean streak, and is fat, strong and takes to beating her. She sends the child out to get a willow switch for the beatings. The stepmother is dogged by a tale of her first husband—he was thawing a frozen valve on a gas drum with a torch when the explosion blew his head off. Some people whispered he'd killed himself to escape his marriage.

Norma becomes largely lost to history. She is replaced by a woman who insists her name is Peggy Lee.

There was also the matter of weather. In 1929, a windstorm leveled half of Bismarck, one hundred miles to the west. Then came the dust storms of the thirties and dust piled up in the home of little Norma Egstrom. Hoboes drifted into town following the tracks.

And the child thinks—or so Peggy Lee long afterward remembered—"I'll leave when I find out where these railroad tracks lead."

*   *   *

I am young standing on the plains and the wind whips across the Dakotas. The old man is gruff with a hand-rolled cigarette barely staying lit, greasy slacks, a torn T-shirt and eyes squinting in the light of day. The towns seem far apart here and lonely as they huddle in the shallow depressions where creeks struggle toward the embrace of the Missouri.

Zig-Zag wheat paper crumpled between his fingers, smoke lazing out his mouth. He looks at the sweep of land with scorn and desire, a conflict known to every person who was driven off the ground by poverty. I walk off into a mown field, stubble punching at the soles of my feet.

Sun a disk roasting the sky.

The towns so small and lonely.

The old man hardly says anything.

But by then he had totally disconnected from the ground in his talk. He was all stocks and bonds and maybe the gold market, and none of this piety of the family farm.

*   *   *

Peggy Lee is in New York during the war. She has left North Dakota, taken a stage name, fallen in and out of love with boys and carved a channel in the world called jazz. Fats Waller has autographed an ace of spades for her. She is singing "That Did It, Marie" one night and Count Basie dances by the bandstand and asks, "Are you sure you don't have a little spade in you, Peggy?"

Lewis and Clark

It is 1794 and Thomas Jefferson writes of a business matter: "There remains on his hands Martin and the Chariot. If the latter cannot be disposed of. . . ." and then Jefferson goes on about wheels. Both are simply property to be sold. Martin has been Jefferson's butler for twenty years but they had an argument and could not come to peace with each other, so Martin asked to be sold. Jefferson peddles his wagon and his man. It is awkward, since Martin's half-sister Sarah, a woman commonly called Sally, has been Jefferson's lover for about ten years. She is the mother of his children and the half-sister of Jefferson's late wife.

Meriwether Lewis of the Corps of Discovery once delivered fifty dollars from Thomas Jefferson to James Callender in hopes of quieting him. This effort failed and Callender's became the poison pen flooding the nation's newspapers with tales of a Black Sally who slept with the author of the Declaration of Independence and bore his children. Callender had been the terror of Richmond, Virginia, for a spell because of his habit of outing white men and their black lovers. Jefferson had brought him on as his secret assassin of opponents in print, and then when he was slow in giving him that postmaster job, the assassin turned on the patron.

Lewis, he went up the river with Clark.

Dakotah

About a quarter of the people who came to this ground were Volga Germans, from colonies planted by Catherine the Great in Russia in order to use German bodies to nail down Russia's claim to the newly conquered steppes. They thrived and then in the latter days of the nineteenth century fled new rules and pressures from the Czar, rules aimed at assimilating the still-German-speaking colonies into the nation.

They came in good part to North Dakota, a fierce place that reminded them of the steppes, a hard portion of the earth whose ways they already knew. They fought learning English, tried to keep their children home and often jerked them from school after the eighth grade. They worked like dogs and built new lives and a new prosperity.

They would arrive in boxcars and that first winter or two live in sod huts, seven, eight, nine, ten to a small, one-room dwelling. The children worked picking up rocks to clear the field. When death came in winter, the body went into the barn until spring, when the roads let neighbors gather for the burying—a body wrapped in a quilt, resting on an old door, the whole thing balanced on buckets lest the mice get to the dead.

The wash went on bushes or barbed wire because clothespins were a luxury. Fly season was hell because no one could afford screens—the baby in its cradle, black with insects.

June meant digging coal for the long winters. Every season meant work.

They survived and stuck.

*   *   *

The house stares down on the empty town and Debra Quarne frowns as she tries to remember who lived there.

"Bublitz," she offers. "I don't know the first name. I know he's dead."

She's fifty-two, has forty-six horses and is the last resident of Hanks. Once there were eight hundred.

"When I was eight or nine," she recalls, "it was empty. When we were kids, we thought it was haunted, had a ghostly feeling. It's like everybody gave up and went away."

Across from her home is a wooden building with missing doors, the Lutheran church where she was baptized. Two hundred yards away is the failed bank—a man hanged himself in the basement there during the dust and ruin of the thirties.

"I love it here," she says. "It's my own little corner of the world."

The dust clouds one blue eye as the severed doll's head stares up in the garage. Nearby is a walker for infants, a red plastic telephone, and two more dolls, one with limbs severed. There is a small newspaper clipping noting the birth of Jolene Melissa, the first child, on October 6, 1982. Also, the sale of a Holstein for $250 in 1974. Fragments of dreams in a garage near a small white frame house with a neighboring red barn in the sweep of the plains. Plus, a small rubber Santa Claus waiting for some holiday.

So many abandoned houses have dolls with blonde hair and blue eyes and no little girls to love them.

The robin's-egg paint breaks into cracks and I keep thinking I can find my life in these ruptures on the surface of the wall. Out the busted window I see the last gasp of the orchard as the trees succumb to abandonment and plains wind. A rusted car sleeps in the tall grass, down the slope the stone footing of the barn is an open mouth of broken teeth, the stove stands free of the kitchen wall, and in the basement bones rest on the floor from beasts seeking hopeless shelter.

Everything is framed in ragged-edge, small photographs, the tiny varnished images from the 1930s when the ground buckled, people sank into their tombs and nothing seemed fresh any longer as dust storms, broken markets and failing lives swept the grasslands.

I keep trying to grab onto something, a scent, a look in the eye, the quiet order of kettles simmering on old stoves with pale green enamel surfaces and that robin's-egg blue always in the background. So many of the abandoned farm kitchens have this color and I am convinced it was the silent protest of women against being there, against their lives, against the sweep of land out the kitchen windows, just as the avocado seed balanced in the empty jelly jar with toothpicks was a tropical flight from northern Januaries and empty bank accounts.

When I was born, every man had his war to tell, every life knew hard times that had been put behind and saw good times that were coming down the pike at the velocity of money. All the stories began with the same line: we had nothing.

Whenever I come into the grasslands I think of him, I feel his hunger for the ground—he'd talk like a drunken poet of the ducks and geese clouding the sky before the wetlands were tiled and murdered—and his contempt for the small futures the plains offered the human soul.

Floating across the grass north of Velva, North Dakota, I

can hear my father's voice and hear footsteps as Eric Sevareid flees the doom of the land. Velva hides in a fold of land
along the banks of the Mouse River safe from the roar of
the plains. The main street is brick and past hopes, a white
bench—1776–1976 and nothing more need be said—by
the old hotel, the Soo Line and grain elevators. Somewhere
nearby, I'm sure, is the hulk of Sevareid's father's failed bank.
The river itself comes down from the Yellow Grass Marshes
of Saskatchewan and eventually turns and flows back into
Manitoba. The ground here is past the edge, the rains go toward Hudson Bay, not New Orleans. The town calls itself Star
City on the Mouse and, maybe, it has a point since nearby
Voltaire does have the river with its meandering course.
A city park laps the banks.

Sevareid cannot stay. The plains seem to chill him. At one
point in his youth, he takes a 2500-mile paddle up to Hudson
Bay and I can't help but feel it was to escape the death grip of
his beginnings on the plains. After that his life was wandering the world reporting on war and ruin.

But my God, buried in his memoirs he caught the feel of
what he fled. It reads like a found poem:

North Dakota.
Why have I not returned for so many years?
Why have so few from these prairies ever returned?
Where is its written chapter in the long and varied Ameri-
    can story?
In distant cities when someone would ask "Where are you
    from?"
and I would answer "North Dakota,"
they would merely nod politely and change the subject,
having no point of common reference.
They knew no one else from there.
It was a large, rectangular blank spot in the nation's
    mind. . . .

Sometimes when galloping a bare backed horse
across the pastures in pursuit of some neighbor's straying
    cattle,
I had for a moment a sharp sense of the prairie's beauty,
but it always died quickly away
and the unattainable places of books were again
more beautiful,
more real.

Velva is a place I feel like parking my life. It is June, the plains rise up green and fresh, the river lazes along, the small houses seem ready for me to move in. Old men sit on benches, flowers leap up from fresh beds, and the taverns beckon with beer signs. My father is down in Cherry County, Nebraska, in the heart of sand dune country. The ground ripples with the waves of sand running east to west and all is coated by grass to disguise the largest dune in the United States. His people tried to make it here in the later part of the nineteenth century but the skies with drought and blizzards drove them away.

He is in a hotel with the rich man in Valentine.

He's spent the day going over his accounts. They have a fine dinner and afterwards they talk.

The man is rich, very rich. He has beaten the sand hills.

He tells my father, "I have wasted my life staying here. Don't you do it."

*   *   *

The Sioux are new men on the plains and they do not even glimpse the Black Hills until around 1770 or 1790—the records are smudged, memories shot by whisky and murder. The grass there is scant for their horses, the game—lions, bears and bighorn—hard to kill. They come briefly for lodge poles and camp just before mountains where the plains can feed their beasts and where the elk and deer come more easily to their bows. Crazy Horse is born in such a place. One big peak is called by the tribe the Hill of Thunder and in 1833 smoke issued from it and the Sioux realized this was the breath of Big White Man. He is buried there and rumbles are the sounds of this white giant. He suffers much, large rocks press against him, all this, the Sioux explain, is his fate for being the original aggressor on their ground.

Sometimes he roams the plains and his prints stretch out at least twenty feet in length. But then he must return to this tomb, the huge rocks pressing on him. Because he is the white who tried to take their land and his pain is a warning to all who have such dreams.

In Bismarck—a name selected by the early land peddlers in the hopes it would attract German settlers—the state capitol was built in the early thirties, a skyscraper that echoes the one Huey Long tossed up around the same year in Louisiana, far downriver. Everything seems smooth now, the horrors of the past all but forgotten. The dusters of the thirties gone, the failure of quarter-section farms long past, the collapse of towns accepted. North Dakota is sitting pretty with oil and gas and coal, with huge farms that make plowboys into paper millionaires and with a population that largely lives in cities on the far eastern edge of the state, where they hunker and pray that they are safe from the wrath of the plains.

Now the pain is distant enough and it can be savored like wars and killings are in motion pictures. At the state historical center in the capitol they've plastered some old moments on the wall where the locals stare out lonely amidst the dinosaur bones and old frocks and hats.

On July 7, 1886, Dr. John Engstad of Grand Forks scratches out an entry in his journal. He carefully notes, "Mrs. Peter Wjoberg, 35, Acton, Minnesota. Has had seven children, two living, five dead. Last spring lost one child after a lung sickness and after that time she has lost considerable weight but her mind has suffered most from melancholia and it is so marked now that she has a staring look, talks to herself. 'I do not sleep,' and sits all day shaking her head. Imagines that her feet will dry up as she asserts there is no circulation in them. Refuses to get well. All organs OK. No pain in back. Tendon reflex almost lost. Very forgetful, forgets to dress or do anything only to sit and meditate."

*　　*　　*

I'm sitting in a lonely house in the snows out on the plains. The woman is quick with her eyes and she has had some hard times in life.

She says, "My father was an alcoholic. He killed himself."

And then recalls how she fixed her old house up, how when she tore out the old plaster she found flax straw for insulation, and at the bottom of the lathe work a foot or more of dust from the big blows in the thirties when the land, all plowed and naked, took to the skies. On a fine May day in 1934, the big blow came right out of the Dakotas and out of Montana also and soon it was a dust storm eighteen hundred miles wide and blowing into New York City and dusting ships at sea. She found that storm sleeping within her walls, an ancient curse now long gone and all but forgotten but still sleeping there within her home and maybe stirring again some day like a creature in a mummy movie.

On January 22, 1899, Emma Ladbury of Gallatin, North Dakota, wrote a friend, "Did you know Mrs. Wilson that used to live near Hope? They were Scotch people. They went to Manitoba a little more than a year ago. Word came a few days ago that she was insane she was at home alone she took the axe and chopped one of her knees through and cut the other limb badly when they came home they found her lying on the ground she had fainted from the loss of blood. She is now in the insane asylum at Brandon, Man. Some say it was religion that drove her insane but I don't think it was."

It is not an accident that the two greatest writers of the plains, Mari Sandoz and Willa Cather, are women. And both left as soon as they could and stayed east and far from the wind and storms and heat and drought and the coarse hands that come from washing clothes with lye and a scrub board. The men seemed committed to dreams of free land, of finding the big rock candy mountain, of independence and fat times, and this commitment spared them from facing the realities of failed crops, hungry children and women dying the slow death of endless births.

Norma Egstrom goes on the road with Benny Goodman's band. She is sixteen years old. Back in Nortonville, she learned two things: one night on an old Atwater Kent radio she picked up Kansas City and Count Basie blew into her mind. And she fell asleep each night listening to the clack of freight trains passing through and picked up a rhythm that underscored her singing. She is seven, and she sings blackfaced in a minstrel act. She turns her back to audiences when she sings. There are tales of her stepmother hitting her with a fry pan, of her showing up at school bruised. Of her dad singing at his railroad job at the station and how this got into his daughter's blood.

Peggy Lee's family kept failing and moving from town to town. North Dakota was seen by its boosters as a place that would host at least two million people. Between 1893 and 1933 they poured in and found a dry plain with violent weather. Some stayed for the nightmare, many fled and all were permanently scarred. The place built on buffalo bones and vacated Indian villages became a walking dead man pretending to be a success. Now the ground has some restored buffalo herds, a last fling at finding a sustainable agriculture here.

Louis L'Amour hails from Jamestown, the place where Peggy Lee's dad ended his faltering railroad career. L'Amour (the family's real name was LaMoore) had a veterinarian dad, and for the time and place lived pretty well. Then he left and wandered and after World War II he invented the West that never existed and that he never found. Every book he ever wrote remains in print and at one point, he fancied building his own western town so he could walk around what he could not find.

Years later the state seeks to paper over the pain of its history and invents a Theodore Roosevelt Rough Rider Award. Two locals who have fled to better spots win: Lawrence Welk and Miss Peggy Lee.

*　　*　　*

A warm breath moves across Wyoming in the winter of 1841, the snow melts on the prairie. And then the temperature plunges once again, the grass becomes imprisoned in ice and the buffalo cannot smash this barrier and reach their feed. Come spring there is not a living buffalo on the grasslands of Wyoming. The plains are endless bones. The beasts never return.

We let this memory go, we bury it deep, we say sixty million buffalo, a hundred million buffalo, a herd of a billion buffalo. There is a place, a home on the range, where the deer and the antelope play, and the sky is not cloudy all day. And never is heard a discouraging word. Lewis and Clark push up the river to discover that passage to the great ocean, and establish a fur trade. Millions will follow their tracks because such is destiny and no one doubts this destination.

Our women will be prim and proper, their hair blonde

and their eyes blue. We will tell everyone this place is the heartland. Eventually our instruments will record a winter day that is sixty below, a summer day that is 121 degrees. We will learn a new word, chinook, for the warm winter wind that can flow over the Rocky Mountains and raise the temperature seventy-five degrees in twenty-four hours. But we will resist what the dead buffalo of Wyoming know.

Momma's gone to dreamland on the train.

* * *

The wall glows a soft blue under a gray sky stalking the brown winter land. A map of the world lies carelessly torn on the jumble of old wood and iron desks. A blackboard stares out with blank eyes at the empty classroom. A shotgun blasts from the field below as men hunt pheasants in the ebbing light. The steps rotted out years ago, one Greek column remains by the entryway, and patches of green shingles cling to the roof. The four-room building sags as it seeps toward the earth. It was thrown up sometime in the 1920s, held grades one through eight, plus high school, and was the pride of Gascoyne.

Originally, the town was Fischbein, North Dakota, but Western Union complained the name required too many dots and dashes and so it became Gascoyne, the handle coming from the railroad foreman that drove the rails here in 1908. There was no frontier here, just empty grassland and then homesteaders. On May 16, 1907, the county got its first newspaper, less than a month later the county was organized, the following year came the railroad and towns were dropped from freight cars like packages tossed off on a siding.

A wind ruffles the tall grass growing by the abandoned building. One classroom has two stoves shoved free of the wall to form a V, the last gesture of home economics. A torn page from a child's exercise book lies next to a fresh pile of dog shit. The instructions ask: "Write the other word."

CRY
AFTER
BAD
ALWAYS

To the north of the old school, buttes rise from the earth. Gascoyne once had maybe two hundred people, was officially designated a city by the state legislature. Now it holds twelve.

Antelope watch from the grass, thousands of pheasants feed in the cut wheat fields and the roll of ground, brown and shivering in the winter light, brings the hooves of buffalo near, herds pounding on the ceaseless journeys from grazed valleys to fresh land, imaginary beasts still here and yet gone. Settlement on this expanse of the plains is barely a hundred years old and already feels over.

I pull into the clean country cafes, the ones with small-type menus always offering liver and onions, the coffee weak, the brew farmers drink morning, noon and night, my aunt serving it in glass cups, the coffee so pale you could study the old pile of Reader's Digests through it, and there is *fleischku-ekle*, and I ask, just what is that? And I'm told, well, you take a hamburger and wrap dough around it and then deep-fry it.

They all believed, every one of them. They got off what they called immigrant cars, a boxcar with the horse, maybe a cow, the family tools and a little furniture, some seed, got off, loaded it on a wagon and rode over the grassland until they got to homestead districts and could file a claim. Every-thing they'd been told by the agents recruiting them, often hired by railroads who need humans along the rails to pro-duce products for the freight, was a lie. The winters came early, the rains not often enough, the locusts rose in biblical scale, the land broke hard to the plow, the price for the crops hardly ever enough, the isolation beyond imagination, the long nights forever, and summer sun exploding in their faces and searing their dreams with flames.

The old lesson plan fluttering and brittle with age by the abandoned school asks for "the other word."

GO
COME

Vernon Peterson, seventy-two, sits with a grizzled beard in the kitchen, his wife pouring coffee, grandchildren underfoot. His father came around 1907, homesteaded, built the sod hut, a life. They were all Norwegians, land hungry, seduced by the promises of the railroad promoters. He now lives in his grandmother's house, the one she moved into after she escaped the sod walls that belched fleas and other insects.

"You stop and think," he offers, "of all the accomplishments there, the joy, the yearning . . . ," and then his voice trails off, the ancestors are near, the sod busting, we're going to whip folk, and now, things have turned out differently.

Gascoyne was going to be the place.

Vern did eight grades in the school. He was raised four miles south, and by god, the school had four rooms, steam heat in radiators, the smell of mittens and scarves and hats drying on the hot metal. He entered a class of two in a school of twelve.

"Farming was a living," he tosses out. "We raised four sons and they all went off to do something else."

His wife says softly, "The sunrises, the sunsets."

Of course the farm of nine hundred acres never worked. He had eleven quarters, each one named after the homesteader that proved them up, bought them, and then failed. Now he is off the land, his nine hundred has been clumped with another large chunk so that the next-generation farmer has a prayer of survival. Even Vern always had a steady job off the land in order to survive.

The school, of course, is a ruin and he faces that fact.

"That's an old landmark," he says. "My sons are going to walk around with their sons and say the old schoolhouse once was here somewhere."

He walks outside. The town is under twenty now, and "that was the grocery, the post office, the general store, the ice cream parlor. Now we've lost our football team to the next town, Scranton, and we may lose the basketball team. We graduated fourteen this year but we only have four in kindergarten."

The sky slate gray hangs like a lid overhead. To the west a narrow band of blue and then the sun drops into this slot and the entire sweep of the plains explodes into orange.

DARK
OVER

Peggy Lee goes back in 1975 to get an honorary doctorate from the University of North Dakota. She finds her past flattened—the tracks torn up, the old depots where she spent her childhood watching her father work either leveled or left to rot.

She tells the press, "I don't know what they did with the various depots, and that made me a little sad because I couldn't find where I was."

Lewis and Clark

The captains are astounded by the relish of the tribesmen for the flesh. But then their own men feed heavily—the crew devours a buffalo, or four deer or one deer and one elk each day. The river runs against the boat, the cold robs their bodies of warmth. Still, the captains see a wonderful country. Clark writes of a "butifull prospect," Lewis says of the river and land "so far as we have yet ascended, waters one of the fairest portions of the globe."

They are camped with the Mandans in the heart of a place that will be named North Dakota. On March 28, 1805, the temperature at sunrise is forty degrees and by afternoon it rises to sixty-four. The river is up one inch, the ice is going out and tumbling down in the froth of the melt are drowned buffalo. And Captain Clark notes, "Few Indians visit us today they are watching to catch the floating buffalo which brake through the ice Crossing, those people are found of those animals tanted and Catch great numbers every Spring."

Outsiders are always stunned by this rite of spring. Charles McKenzie, a Canadian fur trader at the Mandan villages, spells out the nature of this treat: "These dead animals, which often float down the current among the ice for hundreds of miles, are preferred by the natives to any other kind of food: When the skin is raised you will see the flesh of a greenish hue, and ready to become alive at the least exposure to the sun; and is so ripe, so tender, that very little boiling is required—the stench is absolutely intolerable—yet the soup made from it which is bottle green is reckoned delicious."

Decades later, Edwin Thompson Denig trading for furs at Fort Union, near the confluence of the Missouri and Yellowstone, will also mention this dainty.

"Although," he explains, "these drowned animals are so much putrified that the meat will scarcely stick together, and can be eaten with a spoon in its raw state, yet these Indians devour it greedily, even when other and good meat can be had. It is a horrid mess, producing an intolerable stench, and one would think sufficient to cause the worst diseases. Yet they suffer no inconvenience from eating it, which they do, men, women, and children, as much as they can cram down."

Denig is hardly a squeamish outsider. He has two Indian wives and finally leaves the Upper Missouri after decades of trading because he wants his children educated in decent schools in the east.

When he finally scratches out his memoir of his life with the tribes, he practically roars his contempt for how the natives are portrayed: "Hence we find two sets of writers both equally wrong, one setting forth the Indians as a noble, generous, and chivalrous race far above the standard of Europeans, the other representing them below the level of brute creation."

He thinks no one can understand the tribes unless the person lives their lives. And so for over twenty years he does just that. His younger wife, the mother of his children, is named Deer Little Woman and she is an Assiniboine. He dresses her in the best clothes from the east. He also has toys shipped upriver for his children. For himself, there is drink.

"I would also request," he writes his superior downriver,

"as a great favor if you would bring me up a keg say 5 galls of good old Rye, to have the pleasure of drinking your health occasionally. I can hardly look upon myself as the infernal drunkard represented and presume as no accident happened to the 2 g keg of last spring, the 5 g keg will be equally safe."

Dakotah

I stand in a kitchen in southern North Dakota and a man thumbs the town history. He had the farm and then struggled and then he went into pigs and that was good for six years and then in 2002 he says, "We really got a shellacking," and then the farm got sold and the move made into town, the bed and breakfast opened in the house in which he had been born.

"The pheasant hunters," he says, "keep us going."

The pheasant are coming back as the land retires to grass and they have room for their lives. But then, they are immigrants also, brought over from China to enhance the hunt.

His wife pours coffee and says, "I always wanted to marry a farmer."

They have five children, and they are also gone from the land, but, she notes with pride, "they're all in North Dakota," though in the small cities where a future can still be imagined.

An old man reviews his father's life, his life and his sons' lives and then tells me, "They will be the end of it."

Fading white paint on the clapboard, the tiles fallen from the ceiling and now heaped on the floor. Gilmer Anderson, eighty-seven, farms a few miles to the north. He stops his tractor and says, "He went to the home in Mott, what I call the old folks home, and he died there. Rufus Svihovec, Bohemian, you know. He was an awful heavy drinker, married once, the wife died. He was raised a mile and a half west of the house. The place has been empty for years." And then Anderson fires up his tractor and gets back to spreading hay for his cows—he farms alone.

For Ervin Schnieder in Mott, he was Uncle Rufus, a man who worked his father's farm when he was a boy. Rufus had one foot mangled in a mower as a child and lived his life as a cripple. Once just before Ervin went to high school, Uncle Rufus shared some red wine with him—he'd hidden it in the silage—and the next thing Ervin remembered was the cows stepping over him as they entered the barn for milking. The wife, Anna, died in the late sixties, Rufus passed in the early nineties—look at this, says Ervin, and he shows an old black-and-white photograph from the fifties, Anna in the passenger seat, and Rufus leaning over from the wheel with a grin.

When Ervin was a boy, he'd wear new shoes for Rufus to soften them for his mangled foot. He worked as a hired hand, married, liked to drink and then he died. This other photo—the white dress on the wall, the red hat on the mirror—that one Ervin can't place. But he knows it is near Mott, that red hat belongs to the marching band.

"When I was ten," Ervin says, "I saw Uncle Rufus lift the engine from a Model A with his bare hands. Rufus and Anna had a tough life, everyone did then."

I stand outside the visitors' center at Theodore Roosevelt National Park, north unit, and five feet from me a cow buffalo feeds on the green grass of late September. The woolly head does not even lift and the black eyes ignore me. A herd of around 150 shelters in the park that embraces one of Roosevelt's former ranches.

He would come to trade off his North Dakota days and be the cowboy or man of the West. He owned his ranches for fifteen years. All told, by the most generous calculation, he spent maybe 359 days in North Dakota. But he wrote the four-volume history *The Winning of the West*.

Charles McKenzie, an early trader, talks to Hidatsas who are baffled by the whites and their hunger for the hides of beaver.

The tribesmen, he reports, think the whites are sick in the mind: "White people, said they, do not know how to live —they leave their homes in small parties; they risk their lives on the great waters, and among strange nations, who will take them for enemies: What is the use of Beaver? Do they preserve them from sickness? Do they serve them beyond the grave?"

Disney

His brother explains the swing from prairie radicalism to Main Street conservatism this way. Roy Disney writes his folks in 1934 about Upton Sinclair's run for governor of California on the EPIC platform—End Poverty In California. Roy is against the campaign by the muckraker whose novel on the Chicago stockyards and their filth prompted President Theodore Roosevelt to finally pass the Pure Food and Drug Act. He writes, "Many of the things he advocated are going to come around in some way or other. However, I don't believe you can upset society overnight. I can hear Dad saying, 'Now, since the boys have joined the capitalist class and the employers class, they sing a different tune.' Well, it's true."

His brother Walt had a different version of the change. He said when he was a boy in Kansas City Irish kids whose dads worked for the Democratic machine had poured hot tar on his scrotum because his father was a socialist and that incident had made him a "dyed-in-the-wool Republican."

Daniel Boone

The girls are floating in a canoe when they are taken. For days, they endure a forced march north to the Ohio country. One of the girls is the daughter of Daniel Boone and she knows that somewhere behind her he is in pursuit.

They are roasting the hump of fresh-killed buffalo. One girl watches an Indian turn the meat on a spit. She sees blood pour out of his chest before she even hears the shot. Boone's daughter, Jemima, shouts Boone's name.

Soon there is a swarm of men and the girls are rescued. Two of the Indian kidnappers die, the rest vanish into the forest.

Later, they find one of the dead Indians, a Shawnee. Two years later, Boone becomes a Shawnee captive and his owner is the father of that dead man. He becomes Boone's adoptive father.

Jemima for the rest of her life carries an image in her mind: it is midday, the buffalo hump is roasting on a spit, she is exhausted from sleepless nights and endless marching and she glances over and sees her father crawling through the brush to her rescue.

Dakotah

There is a literature about the cold, the wind, the dry spells, the hailstorms, the plagues of locusts, the blizzards, the lightning strikes that kill, of crops destroyed, herds lost in one icy blast, women and men going crazy in the long winter nights, of hunger, loneliness, financial ruin and unanswered prayers.

And yet the ground is beautiful, the horizon constant and distant, the sky blue. The space so generous that the plains swallow up a person and fill one with love and fear at the same instant. The state is pocked with abandoned houses and farms and towns. It is a charnel house of agrarian dreams.

* * *

One Indian woman can dress ten buffalo robes a year. Between 1834 and 1844 the American Fur Company in St. Louis took on about 70,000 robes a year. There is a tumble of numbers written in a clear hand in old ledgers: a steamboat took on 7,000 robes near the Yellowstone and the Missouri in 1833, a North Dakota trading post took in 3,270 robes and 1,140 beaver that same year. This is the magic unleashed by Lewis and Clark.

On March 29, the sun rises with fair weather and it is forty-two degrees. The ice rumbles downriver, the break-up has come and on both sides of the Missouri fires burn on the plains, because Clark records in his notes "it is common for the Indians to Set those Plains on fire near their village for the advantage of early Grass for the hors & as inducement for the Buffalow to visit them."

Already, buffalo are declining east of the river from their former numbers.

In 1738, Pierre Gaultier de Varennes, sieur de La Vérendrye, comes almost to the exact spot where Lewis and Clark winter with the tribesmen in 1804–1805. A native of Quebec, he's fought against the British in New England and shed blood for France in the European wars. But he is mainly a man of the woods and now at age fifty-three he is going to open up a new country for the fur trade and given half a chance he figures to find a way across the continent to the Pacific Ocean. He builds a fort in Manitoba on the portage trail and gives the local Assiniboins presents of powder, ball, tobacco, axes, knives, hatchets and awls. They weep with joy.

He moves with a party of Indians south to what will be central North Dakota. The women and dogs carry the burdens. When he finally arrives at a Mandan village, he finds 130 lodges protected by a palisade and a ditch. And he finds the people already have iron implements even though they are hundreds of miles from the nearest European trading post, even though no one in Europe knows they exist. His guides, the Assiniboins, have been traveling to York Factory on Hudson Bay since the 1680s and trading pelts for tools and in turn trading these to tribes further south for fur. The killing has gone on without anyone even knowing the full pattern—beasts taken down for the hides, and then sold to other natives for iron who in turn take the pelts far north to an outpost on Hudson Bay where they trade for more goods and rare skins travel to Europe and decorate the bodies of other humans who have little or no notion of this hemisphere called Western.

That is why the beginning is so hard to grasp. Wherever the traders go they find iron has preceded them, the beasts have been slaughtered and skinned for this global market. And the locals have sad faces from waves of disease that have also come off the boats and like the iron rippled westward far ahead of the whites.

This is a dreamland where nightmares come without notice. So do the sweet dreams, the knife that holds the edge, the gun that propels the bullet into the body of the beast or of the men and women of other nations. And some of this is instantly grasped, the tribesman are always willing to trade and yet are hostile to the notion of the Europeans selling to their neighbors, an act that would kill their own commercial possibilities and also possibly arm their distant enemies with killing devices.

La Vérendrye is the first part of this wave on the Upper Missouri, the trader who blunders into the place where the knives and guns of his culture have already arrived. He is game, he will lose a son and a nephew and others in his trading probes.

He notes, "This tribe is mixed white and black. The women are fairly good looking, especially the light colored ones; many of them have blond or fair hair."

The rest, that everyone works hard, the lodges are big and tidy, that they sleep naked on a mound of skins. When up and about the men go naked unless wrapped in a buffalo robe, the women likewise save a loincloth a hand wide in front, and so forth, this would not be much commented on. But the naked women, handsome and fair, some blonde, this would ripple through the minds in Europe.

For a half century, no other white man came to the villages. But still tales of the earlier visit lingered.

In 1796, the Missouri Company out of St. Louis sent up a party to latch on to the trade in furs. Along came John Evans, a Welshman, who had journeyed to America in order to use North American fact to shore up European myth. The Welsh believed that a Prince Madoc had discovered America in 1170. When Evans heard stories about the white Indians upriver, he joined the trading group in hopes of finding his kinsman. Other tribes blocked his passage to keep control of the valuable trade goods.

This hunger for finding some other explanation for the place and its people would continue with runic writings, legends, anything but the facts on the ground. Myth would meet myth, beasts and nations come and go, and yet this vapor would rise from the ground like Big White Man protesting his fate underground. When the Americans finally arrived with their myth of Manifest Destiny, their myth of Trees Causing Rain, their myth of fertile soil and verdant farms, their myth of a Cattle Kingdom, a Wheat Kingdom, an Eden kissed by a gold north wind, a place of yeoman farmers following the chapter and verse of Thomas Jefferson, they would join a long cavalcade toward fable, and then will come a winter and then will come the summer with no rain and the winds will rise. It is not that anyone was wrong to come. It was that they were wrong to think their fate would be different.

Men are moving upriver to find a passage to the great ocean, the future is in their eyes, the winter comes and they camp at the Mandan villages full of dreams.

*   *   *

Peggy Lee is back in 1950 for the winter festival as a headliner. The newspaper also notes with pride that four hundred have entered the "Livestock Judging Event." *Look* magazine prints a photo of the hometown girl back in her childhood haunts, an image snapped by a photographer named Stanley Kubrick who will soon give up still images for moving pictures.

When her part in the festival ends, she goes home to see

her dad. Her brother fetches her with a farm truck and they disappear into a blizzard in order to reach her father's deathbed.

She reads him the Twenty-third Psalm:

The Lord is my shepherd: I shall not want:
He maketh me to lie down in green pastures:
He leadeth me beside still waters,
He restoreth my soul . . .

He says, "I never understood that until now."

And he tells her not to bother to come back when he dies. She's got things to do, and he understands. And seven weeks later he is dead.

Peggy Lee does not come back for the burying.

She sits in her living room on a late September day with the temperature dancing in the thirties across the plains. She's about eighty now and one of six human beings left in Corinth, North Dakota, a collapsing town up near the Canadian border.

She has a death book, an old ledger kept from settlement in the early part of the last century until the 1930s. People died a lot of ways—blizzards took a toll and just the normal diseases of life. She's struck by the numbers killed by trains.

Some, of course, are easy to explain, men working the track become statistics in a dangerous trade. But there are others, some mowed down by passing freights, and, then she pauses and lets the thought hang in the air, the notion of someone on a Dakota day stepping in front of a fast freight and leaving this ground behind.

In March 1876, a blizzard trapped a train with two or three hundred people aboard between Fargo and Bismarck. They sat buried in the snows for three weeks. On January 12,

1888, the snows buried barns and houses and killed about a hundred people. Women commonly made breakfast in their farm kitchens wearing hood, shawl and mittens. Sometimes in a bad storm, people would burn parts of their houses in order to stay warm.

It's all in the book, neatly entered by careful hands as the wind blew outside the windows and roared across the plains.

I walk into a bar just a hair south of the Badlands and a woman pours me a drink. Teddy Roosevelt killed his trophy buffalo—that one he'll hang on the wall in Long Island and use the glass eyes—just west of town, over a line into what the folks here now call Montana.

He nails his beast on September 20, 1883, and then the following day cuts off the head and hacks out some meat—possibly using the Tiffany knife he'd brought west for his adventure. He impresses the hands he's hired to guide him because he does not complain.

When he leaves on the 25th, the head goes with him—first making a pit stop at a taxidermist in Bismarck, then traveling on to Roosevelt's home at Sagamore Hill where it still hangs.

He arrives just at the end of the West he seeks. Not only are the buffalo gone from North Dakota that fall, but the world's first rodeo has just been held in Pecos, Texas, a sign that the door is closing on the fable of the region. The Northern Pacific lances through the high plains—one reason for Roosevelt's visit—and the young hunter begins to toy with the notion of commuting from a ranch in the Badlands to his position as a member of the New York Legislature.

All this is a moment of before—that brief period when North Dakota was all about becoming. Now, in Marmarth, it is all about time past in the Pastime Club and Steakhouse. She leans on the bar, one arm bent, smoke in hand, and talk flows about a dying town with life still murmuring all around me. On the wall, a high school photograph from 1939, teachers dressed nice, girls look like virgins, boys dreaming of girls who are not, and off to one side a saddled horse tied to a tree. There are eighty-one people in the old print. The high school is now dead, the people in the photograph scattered. The railroad yard that nourished the town closed in the 1980s.

Patti Perry is the town's economic development officer, a good-sized job for a town of 140 people that once held 2,800. The streets are still lined with brick storefronts and homes. But the life seems to have fled. She says she loves it here, especially the winters, and has never wished to leave.

Here in the bar life continues, Patti talks, and there is laughter in the room. The dinosaurs help. A bed of bones lies a few miles out of town. Just this summer room and board for the field excavation pumped $22,000 into the town's arteries.

"I'm an eternal optimist," Patti allows. "I think the dinosaur field will turn this town around. The hardest part of living in a declining town is to try to figure out how to stop it."

A guy on his way out of the bar pauses to say hello to her.

She asks if he's coming to the burying.

He says, "No, I'm pretty much funeraled up."

After he leaves, Patti notes that the two guys who died were pretty ones, both being in their fifties.

It's nineteen miles to a grocery store, twenty to a doctor. Her family has been here since 1908 and she will never leave. But the town is more than small, it is full of absentees since hunters have bought up a lot of the houses and they're only here for a spell during the season. The rest of the population is largely temporary also—oil field guys probing now that the price is high.

"These things," she sighs, "happen so slowly you really don't notice at first—five leave one year, six the next—and then you wake up one day and wonder what happened here."

To the east a black cloud sweeps across the land, rain roars down, and on the sunny face of this storm a perfect rainbow rides with each end anchored on the ground. The county holds between seven and eight hundred souls, the county seat thirteen people.

Jude and Bo: Part III

He'd promised a niece he would buy her thirty or forty ponies to ride at Rest Haven. He'd promised Bo the November before their marriage that on the next Thanksgiving everything would come from their ground, including the pumpkins for the pie. It took a little longer than he'd figured. But not by much.

By spring 1938, they were in a fourteen-room stone house on 160 acres of pastures, fields, woodland and orchard. The creek ran through the property. There were two big barns, a garage, granary, milk house, hen houses, a small village of buildings huddling on the hill. The soil was mainly clay, and below that the ground became limestone, the rock cut for the house. The house was a large L with kitchen, dining room and parlor on the small part of the L and the huge living room (28 feet by 14) as the pivot. Somewhere against a wall was an upright piano and attached to the back of the L was a wooden extension, a separate living quarters where an old woman lived who tended the kids.

She was called Grandma Deadmore and smelled of vinegar and dust. She kept jars of large salamanders that looked like monsters to my childish eyes. She wrote a diary with nothing recorded but the number of eggs gathered and notices of rain, or lack of rain. She was a creature of the Great Depression, meaning she had no place to live and no way to eat. And so the farm was not slavery but liberation from the cold streets of want.

Jim Rippon was the hired hand at times. And then John became the hired hand. He worked hard but would disappear into the whiskey and vanish for days. Then he'd return, shamefaced and with no real explanation and my father would take him back.

Sometimes the snows were deep and no one could leave for days. But meat hung on hooks in the cellar, the pantry shelves groaned with canned produce from summer, the cows provided milk and butter, there were chickens close by ready for slaughter, and turkeys, geese, ducks and guinea hens. In the kitchen the table was heavy and sheltered by an oilcloth. The dining room centered on a huge oak table. Chests there and in the many bedrooms were black walnut. Mahogany was for other people, save for a carved elephant end table brought back by my uncle Jim from his war in the navy, a thing bought in some African port, I think. The house had these exotic points—ashtrays cut from spent artillery, bayonets, helmets, German loot, the flotsam and jetsam of farm boys thrown in danger and coming back shattered with things in their duffel bags.

Things were simple: wood stove, three-hole privy, hand pump in the yard.

This was Rest Haven.

And everywhere I met odor and scent and fragrance and stench. The dairy herd with piles of cow shit, the acid hitting you in the face as soon as you entered the hen house, the crisp, knifelike odor of the hog pens, the slick shit of the geese and ducks on the grass that would send your feet flying, the dankness coming off the green waters of the creek, the clean scent of the day of creation as cold spring water ran across the stone floor of the milk house where the full cans were chilled. The garden was a tangle of scents, and around the house beds of flowers assaulted. In the spring, when the cherries and apples and pear trees bloomed the air sagged with pollen and pleasure.

The sky is blue, hen houses red, house pale yellow of limestone, the blocks rough with the mark of chisels. No one seemed to know when it was finished, my father simply said it was occupied when Lincoln's funeral train passed at the bottom of the hill on its way to the grave in Springfield.

The bedrooms are always filled with kin and strays, especially during the war and afterward when men hid from their nightmares and sat under the trees talking or in wells of silence. I am the bold toddler and the rebellious child. I take no discipline, I watch everything, and I suck in scent before words and words before speech.

There are candles at Christmas, the smell of cookies, figures that magically emerge from some secret place and act out stories I do not know then and do not believe later. Animals are slaughtered and I watch. Men gather round a steer, the bullet goes through the head, the entrails fall out of the sliced belly into a rusty wheelbarrow, the hoist lifting it, the skinning and then this form dancing in the half light of the barn all red and marbled with white, the cutting and quartering, the cheesecloth wrapped as the corpse cools in the air, the men taking the liver and sweetbreads up to the house, the heavy dark iron skillet hitting the iron castings around the burner, the creaking sound of the hand pump by the sink, then the gush of water, and the smell of liver fills the big kitchen, onions browning, the men having a beer round the table, flies clinging to the screens and out in the yard the cluck of chickens pecking the ground while the sun burns down on the last moisture of morning coming off the hidden dewdrops from the dawn.

There is a radio on, the tubes glowing. I remember years later having a dial stop functioning on one of the big old machines, and looking inside and discovering it reached into the sky because of string that moved it from station to station on a pulley. I was amazed that string could conquer space.

There is a war against hawks and weasels and foxes, one fought ineptly and almost always lost. Bo shoulders the .22 and shotgun. Jude cannot stand to kill, even for his supper. I live in a stream of colors, scents and sounds.

There is the dog. Dick. He is black and white, long fur, survives winter and summer outside and his nose is always in my face.

There is this music of the voices of the women, a song I think I remember because I was so often left with them and out of the workaday way of the men milking, killing, fencing, and plowing.

The women are always doing, the bread kneaded and warming in the wood stove, the smell of hot irons on cloth, milk curdling, eggs warm from just under the hen, seasonings flung in the air as a pot simmers. Their voices never still. Men seem to live outside, and sometimes come through the door, pour coffee and leave again. There is stitching, sewing, knitting, embroidery, crocheting, the click of sticks in some mysterious pattern.

The plane sliding down the board, wood curling up, the oil rich in the air coming off the blade just freshened, the knobs on the plane blood-rich with the look of rosewood, the steady sound—half slice, half scrape—the board going level.

She smiles down at me as I squat on the floor. There is always the same light, the rich flow of afternoon, cows milked, eggs gathered, a list of tasks written in her skull, and there were so many men and women at the farm they all swirl together in laughter, scent and soft breasts and strong hands and arms, women hiking their legs up as they fastened their garters to their nylons and tossed me smiles.

Hogs at the trough, Poland-China, all black and white and fat, my Uncle Reddy feeding them as they jostle for place, and my father years later telling me you can go down the line when they are feeding and slice their throats and the neighbor will not even pause in his feasting until he feels that blade. I wade into them, their warm bodies rubbing against me.

The hand-cranked corn grinder, its iron a rusty red as it stands mounted on a stout fence post under slate-gray sky, and feed spilling into a pail while all around the white chickens are underfoot. The geese already terrify me. Turkeys, too.

I remember one night Uncle Reddy arguing about his hogs, I don't remember the matter at hand, just that he thought they should earn more for their keep. Lucille cut the cards and he calmed. I can still hear the sound of the chips hitting the top of the oak table, clack, clack, clack. The low tones as the cards flew out, the ashtrays filling and the drinks being refreshed against the dawn that always comes.

They have Rest Haven. Reddy comes and goes and then they buy ten acres, prime with white oak across the road, and he can go there and have his own country.

I stare at the old photographs, willing the ground back into my life. There are dozens of them in the same box with the neatly tied love letters. The land flowing down the hill, huge oaks, the stone of the farmhouse, the pump forlorn in the winter yard. Years later, the old man tells me he had planned to be buried in the front yard and here it is, several acres of grass, oak, and orchard rolling down the hill to the road. And all this ends suddenly.

In the spring of 1948, Jude writes to his brother Reddy that he is moving to a flat in Chicago, that he plans to sell the farm within five years, that he is splitting up the property so that Reddy can live on the ten acres and the farm can be sold piecemeal—the house separate from the land—or as a unit. The letter is terse, exact, and final.

The next photograph in the box is of me playing football on concrete in a Chicago alley lined with brick garages. I hated every minute of city life but I never asked my father why we left the farm. My mother said the commute was getting too hard for him, but even as a child I wondered at this explanation since he had made that commute for ten years, even bought an army surplus jeep so that he could batter through the snows to the train station.

I remember loud kitchen arguments between him and his brother Reddy, scenes where I was barred from the room.

I find a letter written by my Aunt Lucille, the cupid that put together Jude and Bo and launched the fantasy called Rest Haven. It is very long and very clear. I am stunned to find that my aunt could write something as harsh and plain as a legal brief. She, like her brother Jude, was part of the glue that held the brothers and sisters together in the face of their father Sam's intemperate ways and violent spells.

My grandfather's obituary in 1943 shows her hand: "He was always kind to down and outers and would share the last crust of bread with one less fortunate than he. He believed in living and letting other folks live also and always found some good in everyone. He had good principles and even though he expressed them in a rough way his children will never forget his teachings. He wanted to be independent and not be a burden to his family. So he was ready to go. His last stroke a week and a half ago left him blind so death spared him many lonely hours. He had a keen mind which was alert to the last. He kept up with the news by radio and had definite ideas about the times as he was politically minded."

Now she must compose a different kind of history. She begins in this letter to Jude and Bo, "I suppose this letter will be the hardest one I'll ever have to write—sincerely hope so. First, Bo, let me tell you that one of our family has caused you the grief that I know you feel."

Reddy has been telling family members for years that Bo was trying to kill Jude by keeping him well supplied with drink. Or he has been telling family members for years that Bo was slipping poison in Jude's food and slowly killing him that way. My father has batted off these statements, almost pretended not to hear, so that he could keep a relationship with his brother. I have never found a single photograph of my uncle in which he was smiling. He always has his legs apart as if ready to wade into a fight. And of course, he always was ready. He had beaten men near to death, been jailed on attempted murder, wandered up and down that Mississippi River playing cards in the back rooms for high stakes. My mother's wedding ring came from such a game and my father bought it from his brother.

Lucille reviews the facts: the years of increasingly bizarre behavior, the visits to doctors in various states, the fact that the condition is incurable because of what she calls a "germ." The word is never spelled out but it is clear all the same: syphilis. My uncle's brain is being slowly devoured by some night or afternoon of pleasure he had long ago on the river. Dr. Stevenson agrees. So there is nothing to debate.

Rest Haven has become a hell.

But what has surfaced is not really syphilis, it is a reck-lessness in the blood and I recognize this fact. No one in my family has ever held ground. Richard Bowden came back from his war and left Minnesota for the sandhills of Nebraska and then went upriver to the Dakotas and then back to Iowa and finally died penniless, married to a very young girl so that she could fatten on his Civil War pension.

Sam Bowden has been a diligent ne'er-do-well, often too drunk in the morning to successfully milk the goats he kept to help feed his swarm of kids. None of his children managed to stick on a real piece of ground.

The syphilis is an old family friend. When Charlie died in the insane asylum in the early thirties at Cherokee, Iowa, the family spoke of his gassing in World War I and how he had to be locked up after he went at his mother with a hoe. The obituary recalled his military service and that of his brothers and then added, "Like many another this lad was wounded in mind, weakened till his heavy eyelids fell in the sleep that knows no awakening."

But what the family did not say out loud was what they believed: that germ, syphilis.

And now it is back.

The farm is sold in the early fifties, Jude continues to run Reddy's finances by registered mail. He lives ten miles from his brother and never speaks to him again.

Jude buys 212 acres of woodland and swamp in Wisconsin, lives sometimes in a trailer there without a well, a phone, or electricity.

Then he shifts to a new notion: a series of campers he fashions himself and he vanishes for weeks at a time into the American hinterlands.

After Rest Haven moved beyond his grasp, he bought a two-flat in Chicago, put that big work table in the basement in a kind of alcove next to the two large tanks that held oil for the furnace, a change from coal that delighted him as if he were being liberated from some slave camp full of coal dust and spent clinkers that must be removed. The big table had an array of tools rescued from the farm, and an anvil and vise of industrial scale. His kit of memories, I suspect. And that is where he hung the oil paintings in gilded gold frames of cows grazing in pastures, the sky blue, sun warming the land, there he kept fragments of the land he no longer possessed.

I would go down there at night to oil my rifle as a boy, my .22 bolt-action with a clip, and the cows would watch me.

I would ask why they were kept down there in their frames.

My father would tell me, "They don't belong in the city."

Dakotah

John James Aubudon comes into possession of a golden eagle trapped by a New Englander. It is 1833 and he is living in Boston. He is captivated by the bird's vitality and entertains the idea of releasing it after he finishes his painting. But he struggles to draw it from life and finds the bird, a female three feet long with a seven-foot wingspan, resistant to his goals of art. The eagle refuses to remain motionless. So he sets it in a room with a smoldering pan of charcoal in the hope the smoke will kill it. The eagle lives. Next, he adds sulfur to the charcoal. The eagle lives.

So he stabs it in the heart.

The painting takes sixty hours over a two-week period and earns Audubon enduring fame as a man who knows nature and captures its wild freedom. In it, the eagle is portrayed killing a hare.

"I'm the oldest man in town," he says. "I was born in 1911, twelve miles north on a homestead. We lived in a sod house, it wasn't very big, there were seven of us. My father came from Norway, he was heading for Wisconsin when he found he had TB, so we stayed here where it was dry. He died when I was two.

"I can't imagine where my mother found the food. We had 160 acres, my father broke sod with four oxen. I can remember when we didn't have a privy, we had to go east of the house to the ash pile and crap. There wasn't much excitement—but we had a sled.

"I went eight grades to a country school. Nobody my age ever went to high school—we had to work. I worked for a neighbor at age eight picking up rocks in the field all day.

"That house with the cat? It used to belong to some people from Montana, been empty at least fifty years. They hauled it over here, a man and a woman. Their kids were already on their own. They farmed a little bit. What happened to them? I dunno, I suppose they got old and croaked.

"I got my own farm in '36, ended up with twelve quarters I plowed with horses. I put up seven buildings. We had seven gallons of cream every other day. In '36, we didn't have any rain at all. In '36 with the dusters, it was so dark you couldn't see anything inside the house, everthing just blew away. You had to get used to breathing dirt.

"In '34 we found coal on our land, I'd haul it into Grenora when it was forty below for twenty cents a ton. I got married in '36, she was Norwegian, too. Our first baby was a girl, stillborn. Do you know what stillborn means? We had two boys.

"In '39, I got 25 cents a bushel for my crop—it wasn't enough to make a payment on a free lunch.

"I've still got my hair. I've had a good life, a lovely wife. She died seven years ago. I'm alone. You know I sit here alone for six months at a time, nobody comes to see me. I've outlived them all.

"It's ten above zero, ten above, ten above.

"I'm the oldest man in town."

The railroad comes in the fall of 1907 and by 1908 Marmarth is a tent city going to wood and brick. The first high school class graduates in 1912. North Dakota has almost no frontier moment—it goes from high grassland to settlement with the unloading of lumber off trains and the swing of hammers. Six passenger trains a day come through, along with many freights. The roundhouse employs the men and by 1915 a thousand people cluster here under newly installed electric lights. Natural gas is piped into businesses and homes by 1917, and the next year come water and sewer connections. Main Street is two banks, two hotels, a hardware store, meat market, theater, gas station, Ford dealer, jewelry store, laundry, post office, hospital and the town sports a newspaper, the *Marmarth Mail*. By 1916, a bridge crosses the Little Missouri. The Mystic Theater opens in 1914.

In some ways the anchor of the town's identity is the Barber building, first thrown up in 1909, then rebuilt in 1918 after a fire. The two-story brick hulk still dominates the corner of the main street. Like much of the town, the railroad station, the old bunkhouse for workers, is empty now. The Mystic Theater is owned by the local historical society and hosts a spree of cowboy poetry each summer.

Outside of town is a huge metal sculpture of a dinosaur. Ancient bones now seem like the ticket to the future.

Daniel Boone

In the 1780s and '90s, Daniel Boone becomes a success and falls into the failure of normal life. His biography comes out in 1784 and soon a backwoods legend becomes an international celebrity. Thomas Jefferson on his mission in Paris reads of one Daniel Boone. Lord Byron fits him into his long poem, *Don Juan*.

Boone is the businessman, the surveyor, the land speculator. He watches the game beat away, the tribes falter and then leave. He is the man who has lost a brother and two sons to Indians. He is the man said to own either a hundred thousand acres or thirty-one thousand acres of Kentucky. He keeps moving, opens a tavern, wheels and deals.

When it is over, he will not own a square foot in Kentucky. When it is over, the great paradise of the wilds that seduced him will be gone. When it is over, he will die.

Dakotah

The town of Corinth is down to three families, fewer than ten souls. Up on the hill were the rock rings of fifty tepees, but then his father tore them up and threw the stones in a coulee. The early settlers hauled buffalo bones to Williston to sell for fertilizer, called it the Bone Trail. His father came over from Norway in 1905. Fifty-three years later he decided to visit his four sisters back in the home country, but he had no papers, he'd never bothered to become an American citizen. One woman from his father's town had come over, met a man in New York and married. Then the man died and she returned home rich. So the recruiters told the immigrants, come, in America you will all be millionaires.

Melvin Wisdahl is past eighty and the dying town follows the arc of his life. He remembers when it had almost a hundred people. And he remembers what most want to forget.

There were a lot of kids when he was young and not much money and no roads. In the twenties, the KKK was big in the area, nearby Wildrose had three hundred people and a hundred came for a Klan rally. There were hardly any blacks, so the Klan focused on Catholics. A man rode in on horseback, murdered a family in the area, and was lynched. The man who dropped the rope was from West Virginia, six foot eight.

His aunt married a man who drank and had a mean streak. Then she got the cancer and went off and drank poison. Her one daughter became a schoolteacher, came home from Williston one night and all was well, and then the next day she took strychnine. Depressed. The father died drunk. One son died in a chemical fire in Pittsburgh during World War II. One daughter became treasurer of the Alaskan Railroad. Another daughter slit her wrists out in California in the fifties. They were all very bright, but sad.

The town shrank and tumbled in on itself. He and his wife, Morrene, made some good crops, raised two boys and loved farming.

Melvin can still find a buffalo wallow he first saw seventy years ago as a boy, one with a big granite rock in the middle. Of course, the rock is not so high now, the erosion has slowly filled the wallow and licked against the sides of the stone.

The empty is always there to fill some hole in those who come. The tribes find buffalo, get the horse and build both a life and a belief in the eternal trueness of this life. And then in less than two centuries they are broken and the buffalo is bones. The ranching frontier begins in 1883 when the first substantial herds of Texas longhorns arrive and ends in the winter of 1886–1887 when the breath of the place kills the beasts in place.

Roosevelt salts his cattle dreams with $82,500—he'd inherited from his father $125,000 plus another $62,500 when his mother died on Valentine's Day, 1884. His herds grow and finally reach somewhere between thirty-five hundred and five thousand—he never really knows himself. He invests in land. He squats, throws up some buildings and plans to get rich off government land and free grass.

After the blizzards of that winter of '86–'87, he makes a visit and pens a note to his sister: "I'm bluer than indigo about the cattle. It is even worse than I feared; I wish I was sure I would not lose more than half the money ($80,000) I invested out here. I am planning to get out."

He sputters along with his crushed holdings until 1901 when his prospects get better—someone shoots the president and TR gets the job and a fine salary.

In the eastern part of the state, bonanza wheat farms with hundreds of hands and thousands of acres come in the seventies and then are smashed by lower grain prices in the eighties. After that come the waves of settlers in the aughts and teens of the new century. They swallow the Dust Bowl, flee to World War II jobs and after that comes the long sigh of North Dakota contracting in human numbers.

The light glares on the snow as a hundred pheasants explode into the sun with a thrum of wingbeats near Bethel Lutheran Church. The white building with steeple went up around 1912 and for years the mural of Christ behind the pulpit and pink walls of the sanctuary greeted the faithful. Numbers fell in the fifties and the congregation of twenty-five or thirty joined with one in nearby Wildrose. But it was hard.

Dennis Jacobson, fifty-seven, explains. "For a few years, we had church just in summer. It was a way to close it down but not too suddenly. Then for a few years, once a summer. There was a group of people, and my father was one, who decided they wanted to keep it up rather than let it go to ruin."

Recently, they spent eight or nine thousand dollars repairing the steeple.

But Dennis advises, "This will probably be the last time there will be money spent."

The church on the country road is surrounded by graves with headstones expressing love for mothers and fathers and children.

Near Sheyenne a continental divide sign sits by the two-lane road. The tilt now goes toward Hudson Bay. Behind me is Jamestown, a way station for Peggy Lee in her voyage out of the plains and into jazz. Sheyenne itself is small, huddled and has the feel of so much of the plains, of falling in on itself and eventually vanishing. It feels like the northern edge of the world but once it was the southern edge. The Metis, half-castes who took up the Catholic church, European dress and, to a degree, the market economy, built real houses, did a buffalo hunt each year out on the plains accompanied by priests, designed the Red River cart with two huge, solid wooden wheels. They became what Europeans had always claimed to desire from Indians, a people willing to come into the fire, take up settled ways and set aside ancestral gods. For a spell, settlers heading from Ontario to the hoped-for new wealth of the Canadian plains had to come through Chicago, St. Paul and these parts, this long roundabout route all an effort to escape the morass left by a glacial footprint called the Laurentian Shield. And so this region of Metis became the destination for those dreaming of a Canadian breadbasket on the plains. They flourished just north of here until the Dominion of Canada came after the American Civil War and crushed them in Canada's one and only Indian war because, in the face of blatant discrimination, they sought self-rule. It was a strange war with sharpshooter Metis mowing down Canadian troops and at the same time simply trying to farm and be left alone, a war where their leader marched into battle clutching not a gun but a giant cross and where after one combat the Canadian commander found a dead ninety-three-year-old Metis in a rifle pit.

The Metis scatter, some into the United States, some into deceit. Their leader, Louis Riel, is hanged by the neck until dead in the early 1880s. In 1896, a young officer named Lieutenant John J. Pershing leads a group of buffalo soldiers on a manhunt for Metis refugees and ships fifty-three back to Canada.

I go down to Devil's Lake and it is rising. The town huddles and worries about flooding. For centuries the cycle of the landlocked basin has been simple—about every two hundred years the lake gets huge, floods everything, then cuts a channel to the Sheyenne River, drains away into the Red and disappears into Canada. None of this mattered until they built the town of Devil's Lake (the name a misunderstanding by early priests of the Indian handle, which was Spirit Lake).

I am talking to a woman and she is Lakota and her husband of the Norwegian tribe. They tell me their son has lost his business once and his home twice as the waters rise.

They seem unconcerned since it is the way of the land.

Whitecaps form on the lake as the wind whips across the shallow pan of water.

Daniel Boone

Boone hunts. He is in his sixties, he is bedeviled by debt and lawsuits. Kentucky has people claiming twice as much land as actually exists there and Boone as a surveyor is constantly dragged into court. Even Henry Clay, then a rising attorney, sues him. His property melts away. The old man hunts.

He moves up on the Big Sandy, and lives with his wife and two daughters and their husbands in shacks. They eat from rough trays, use a bench for a table, share a butcher knife and use cane spliced with tines as forks. Boone kills 155 bears in a season. He boils the fat for oil, sells the meat and hides. Arthritis freezes him up and often his wife must carry his rifle in the woods.

He has given his life to Kentucky, he is the famous man, and now he is a financial ruin, a hunter with a failing body. And uncomplaining. In his last years he said that he had never sought "empire, or rule, or profit."

In 1798, with a warrant out for him, he leaves with his kin. First, he helps topple a poplar and then they fashion a dugout fifty or sixty feet in length, five feet in diameter that can haul five tons. Daniel Boone crosses out of the United States into Spanish territory and settles on Femme Osage creek just off the Missouri River. The soil is rich, the game thick, and tribesmen still thrive nearby. Boone said after he left Kentucky, broke and at the mercy of creditors, that he would rather have his head cut off than ever set foot in the state again. And by all trustworthy accounts he never returned.

He wanders. There are tales of the old man crossing the plains, of dropping in on the Great Salt Lake. In 1810, at about age seventy-five, he joins a party, goes upriver, sees the Rocky Mountains and the Yellowstone country.

He is forever in motion.

Boone dies in 1820.

Delta

I am in a delta juke joint and I am drunk and I am the only white person. The air is humidity and smoke and the river flows less than a mile away. The music is solid blues, simple lines repeating with a sameness that echoes the river itself.

Bix Beiderbecke during his headlong plunge into the bottle and early death puts down his horn and explains, "One of the things I like about jazz, kid, is I don't know what is going to happen next. Do you?"

My aunt from Louisiana wound up working a sewing machine in a sweatshop near the coking ovens and refineries of Joliet, Illinois. She had a bed of peonies near a small wooden house in a sliver of woods and taught me to make a cross in front of the eyes of white chickens held to the ground, an act that hypnotized them, and then she cut their throats. I can still smell the wet feathers as I plucked the birds. Just as I can smell the heat of the night on the delta of the Mississippi as the car slices toward the river between the cotton fields and a woman rich in scent nuzzles my ear as I guzzle moonshine and dream on.

Dakotah

June number nine for me and I slide into Strasburg North
    Dakota
Clouds breaking up
Buttes left behind at Linton
Wheat creeping green out of the wintered fields
Sloughs
The land flattens
And on Main Street
Two people paint warning curbs a screaming yellow.
Shiela's café hosts a table
Of seven old women and one man.
The signs over the kitchen
Say
Remember Yesterday
And Cherish Tomorrow
or
Wish It
Dream It
Do It.
Two miles of gravel road lead me to the Lawrence Welk
    homestead.
The sign directing visitors is almost obliterated by
    gunshots.
The shelterbelt of trees, dead or dying.

A mannequin holding an accordian stands in the hayloft of
the barn.

The house seems so small.

No one else is here.

Lawrence and the Champagne Lady left long ago.

The building is posted: Ludwig and Christiana Welk's home.

Blackbirds huddle in the windbreak.

A bus parked in the yard says KEEP A SONG IN YOUR
HEART.

Two tiny buildings claim to be a granary and workplace for
a blacksmith.

I feel a before. I feel an after. But I can feel nothing past
after.

Lewis and Clark

On June 4, 1804, Clark is on the Missouri and his men kill seven deer. One man thinks he found lead ore. Clark describes the ground as "good 2nd rate land."

But he can't forget the night before.

A bird sang "all last night and it is the first of the kind I ever herd."

He calls it a nightingale, a species unknown in the US.

No one has ever identified the bird and the song that bewitched the captain through the dark hours.

Jude and Bo: Part IV

When my father's firstborn comes he toys with naming him Land.

There is only one photograph in the pile of old snapshots that matters to me. I am two, it is winter, the cold steps leading into the stone house are in the background. I wear a knit cap, a scarf and heavy jacket. I sit on the ground oblivious of snow and winter. My right hand strokes Dick, rubs his black and white fur.

The day Jude and Bo left the farm, just as we finished loading up the car, Dick vanished.

They would go back repeatedly to see if he turned up.

He never did.

They both saw this as a mystery.

I am no coward, but I am so strong;
it is so hard to die.

MERIWETHER LEWIS, former personal
secretary of President Thomas Jefferson
and later governor of Upper Louisiana
Territory, dying at sunup in Tennessee, an
apparent suicide, October 11, 1809. Later,
his friend Alexander Wilson, the first great
American ornithologist, went to the area
and paid for a fence to keep hogs from dis-
turbing his remains.

I'm going now. My time has come.

DANIEL BOONE, dying, Femme Osage
Creek, Missouri, September 26, 1820

Notes

13   *Our conduct toward these people*: Jon Meacham, *American Lion: Andrew Jackson in the White House* (New York: Random House, 2008), 122–123.

13   *It was then in the depths of winter*: Meacham, *American Lion*, 151–152.

15   *Advertisement for Runaway Slave*: Meacham, *American Lion*, 302–303.

15   No use for you to cry: Fats Domino, "Walkin' to New Orleans," United Artists XW 007, "The Silver Spotlight Series" (Domino/Bartholomew/Guidry), Travis Music Co. BMI.

17   *Captain William Clark jots down his new world*: Clay S. Jenkinson, ed., *A Vast and Open Plain: The Writings of the Lewis and Clark Expedition in North Dakota, 1804–1806* (Bismarck: State Historical Society of North Dakota, 2004), 37–38.

18   *That is the way the Arikaras*: Douglas R. Parks, ed., *Myths and Traditions of the Arikara Indians* (Lincoln: University of Nebraska Press, 1996), 313–314.

27   *It may be doubted whether there are many other animals*: David R. Montgomery, *Dirt: The Erosion of Civilizations* (Berkeley: University of California Press, 2007), 13.

29   *Sixty-five million years ago, a meteor*: Tim Flannery, *The Eternal Frontier: An Ecological History of North America and Its Peoples* (New York: Atlantic Monthly Press, 2001), 147–151.

31   *I am a pilgrim and a stranger*: Joseph G. Rosa, *They Called Him Wild Bill: The Life and Adventures of James Butler Hickok* (Norman: University of Oklahoma Press, 1974), 19–20. Spelling and punctuation in the letter corrected.

31   *Martha Canary, better known as Calamity Jane*: James D. McLaird,
      Calamity Jane: The Woman and the Legend (Norman: University of
      Oklahoma Press, 2005), 24–25.

32   *He becomes a man with many tales attached*: Rosa, *They Called
      Him Wild Bill*, 10, 16, 234.

42   *When he dies in 1888*: Alice C. Fletcher and Francis La Flesche,
      The Omaha Tribe, Volume Two (Lincoln: University of Nebraska
      Press, 1992 [1905–1906]), 631–634.

69   *There is on the globe one single spot*: James Worsham, "Jefferson
      Looks Westward," *Prologue Magazine*, Winter 2002, vol. 34, no. 4,
      National Archives and Records Administration, archives.gov
      /publications/prologue/2002/winter/jefferson-message.html.

73   *Well, even if it is*: Bill Crow, *From Birdland to Broadway: Scenes
      from a Jazz Life* (New York: Oxford University Press, 1993),
      149–153.

73   *You take each solo like it was the last one*: Steven A. Cera, "Pee
      Wee Russell: A Singular, Scintillating & Shuddery Style," *Jazz Pro-
      files* (blog), October 20, 2017, jazzprofiles.blogspot.com/2017/10
      /pee-wee-russell-singular-scintillating.html.

75   *tell you the pitch of a belch*: Jean Pierre Lion, *Bix: The Definitive
      Biography of a Jazz Legend* (New York: Continuum, 2005), 4–7.

78   *Boone was very profligate*: John Mack Faragher, *Daniel Boone:
      The Life and Legend of an American Pioneer* (New York: Henry
      Holt and Company, 1993), 29, 31, 48.

80   *As a boy he catches an owl*: Neal Gabler, *Walt Disney: The Triumph
      of the American Imagination* (New York: Random House, 2007
      [2006]), 207.

80   *Say we open with morning in the forest*: Gabler, *Walt Disney*,
      320–321.

81   *He's hunting for his mother*: Gabler, *Walt Disney*, 336, 396–397.

89   *In the country is the idea of home*: Robert G. Ingersoll, "Abraham
      Lincoln, 1894," in *The Works of Robert G. Ingersoll*, Dresden
      Memorial Edition, Vol. XII, 245–255 (Ingersoll League, 1929).

92   *Other visitors also take a toll*: Fergus M. Bordewich, *Killing the
      White Man's Indian: Reinventing Native Americans at the End of
      the Twentieth Century* (New York: Doubleday, 1996), 178–179.

93   *In those hours before dawn*: Faragher, *Daniel Boone*, 63, 79–80.

93   *He finds an old Indian in the forest*: Robert Morgan, *Boone: A Biog-
      raphy* (Chapel Hill, NC: Algonquin Books, 2007), 116–117.

93   *Captain Caspar Mansker hears an alarming sound*: Morgan, *Boone*, 120.

96   *In 1834–1835, this harvest*: Donald J. Wishart, *The Fur Trade of the American West, 1807–1840* (Lincoln: University of Nebraska, 1992 [1979]), 58.

96   *a toehold on the plains felt like this*: William C. Sherman and Playford V. Thorson, eds., *Plains Folk: North Dakota's Ethnic History* (Fargo: North Dakota Institute for Regional Studies, 1988), 8.

96   *Or it is 1884 and the Northern Pacific Railroad*: Sherman & Thorson, *Plains Folk*, 10–11.

96   *There were days*: Eric Sevareid, *Not So Wild a Dream* (Columbia: University of Missouri Press, 1976 [1946]), 5.

100   *But a dog found him in the woods*: Morgan, *Boone*, 121–122.

108   *Norma becomes largely lost to history*: Peter Richmond, *Fever: The Life and Music of Miss Peggy Lee* (New York: Henry Holt and Company, 2006), 16–17.

109   *Count Basie dances by the bandstand*: Richmond, *Fever*, 111.

110   *It is 1794 and Thomas Jefferson*: Annette Gordon-Reed, *The Hemingses of Monticello: An American Family* (New York: W. W. Norton, 2008), 486–489.

114   *North Dakota. Why have I not returned for so many years?*: Sevareid, *Not So Wild a Dream*, 5.

116   *Sometimes he roams the plains*: Edwin Thompson Denig, *Five Indian Tribes of the Upper Missouri* (Norman: University of Oklahoma Press, 1961), 5–6.

116   *On July 7, 1886, Dr. John Engstad*: Elizabeth Hampsten, *To All Inquiring Friends: Letters, Diaries, and Essays in North Dakota, 1880–1910* (Grand Forks: Department of English, University of North Dakota, 1980), 270.

119   *A warm breath moves across Wyoming*: Ibid.

123   *I don't know what they did*: Richmond, *Fever*, 368.

124   *The captains are astounded*: David Lavender, *The Way to the Western Sea: Lewis and Clark across the Continent* (Lincoln: University of Nebraska Press, 2001 [1998]), 159.

124   *butifull prospect*: Ibid., 181.

124   *Few Indians visit us today*: Jenkinson, ed., *A Vast and Open Plain*, 253.

124   *These dead animals*: Ibid.

125   *these drowned animals*: Denig, *Five Indian Tribes of the Upper Missouri*, 49.

125   *Hence we find two sets of writers*: Ibid., xxx–xxxi.

125   *I would also request*: Ibid., xvi.

129   *White people, said they*: Jenkinson, ed., *A Vast and Open Plain*, 26.

130   *His brother Walt had a different version*: Gabler, *Walt Disney*, 448.

131   *Jemima for the rest of her life*: Morgan, *Boone*, 208–213.

132   *One Indian woman can dress ten buffalo*: Elwyn B. Robinson, *History of North Dakota* (Lincoln: University of Nebraska Press, 1966), 94.

133   *it is common for the Indians*: Jenkinson, ed., *A Vast and Open Plain*, 253.

136   *Peggy Lee does not come back*: Richmond, *Fever*, 181–183.

136   *In March 1876, a blizzard*: Robinson, *History of North Dakota*, 168.

148   *The painting takes sixty hours*: Greg Cook, "Audobun in Boston," The New England Journal of Aesthetic Research (website), January 27, 2007, gregcookland.com/journal/2007/01/audubon-in-boston_27.html.

153   *I'm bluer than indigo*: Roger L. Di Silvestro, *Theodore Roosevelt in the Badlands: A Young Politician's Quest for Recovery in the American West* (New York: Walker & Company, 2012), 90.

157   *He has given his life to Kentucky*: Faragher, *Daniel Boone*, 322.

ABOUT THE AUTHOR

Author of many acclaimed books about the American Southwest and US–Mexico border issues, CHARLES BOWDEN (1945–2014) was a contributing editor for *GQ*, *Harper's*, *Esquire*, and *Mother Jones* and also wrote for the *New York Times Book Review*, *High Country News*, and *Aperture*. His honors included a PEN First Amendment Award, Lannan Literary Award for Nonfiction, and the Sidney Hillman Award for outstanding journalism that fosters social and economic justice.

ABOUT THE AUTHOR OF THE FOREWORD

TERRY TEMPEST WILLIAMS is writer-in-residence at the Harvard Divinity School. Her many books include *Refuge: An Unnatural History of Family and Place*, *The Hour of Land: A Personal Topography of America's National Parks*, and most recently, *Erosion: Essays of Undoing*. She is a member of the American Academy of Arts and Letters as well as a recipient of a Lannan Literary Fellowship and a John Simon Guggenheim Fellowship. She divides her time between Castle Valley, Utah, and Cambridge, Massachusetts.

Bowden, Charles, 1945-2014
Dakotah